# A
# ROCK
# AND
# A
# HARD
# PLACE

# A
# ROCK
# AND
# A
# HARD
# PLACE

*How to Make Ethical*
*Business Decisions When*
*the Choices Are Tough*

## Kent Hodgson

## amacom

American Management Association

This publication is designed to provide accurate and authoritative
information in regard to the subject matter covered. It is sold with
the understanding that the publisher is not engaged in rendering
legal, accounting, or other professional service. If legal advice or
other expert assistance is required, the services of a competent
professional person should be sought.

Library of Congress Cataloging-in-Publication Data

Hodgson, Kent.
    A rock and a hard place : how to make ethical business decisions when
the choices are tough / Kent Hodgson.
        p.  cm.
    Includes bibliographical references and index.
    ISBN 0-8144-5037-7
    1. Business ethics. 2. Decision-making (Ethics) I. Title.
HF5387.H63  1992
658.4'08—dc20                                               91-40912
                                                                  CIP

Printing number

10  9  8  7  6  5  4  3  2  1

To my mother,
**Ruth Kent Hodgson,**
who supported me with love and
confidence during the years of
writing, only to die within weeks
of the book's completion

# Contents

# Preface

The most critical professional task you have is making decisions. If you want to make better decisions, this book is for you. Better, more consistent, and more effective choices are your payoff.

Personal and organizational success is a direct result of good decisions, and better decision making in a complex and changing organizational world is a difficult challenge today.

Most of your decisions have two factors in common: They flow from values and principles you hold, and they are aimed at doing something. What you really do is more complicated than it may seem, and it can best be described as value-based decision making for action. While immensely important and difficult, value-based decision making can become easier and better.

I've spent the last ten years listening to, consulting with, and training executives, managers, salespeople, and other organizational professionals around the United States. Whatever they studied was applied to making better and more effective decisions. Working with them has given me two insights about organizational life today, and these insights provided the impetus for writing *A Rock and a Hard Place*.

First, as you make choices for action, is the importance of considering stakeholders—the ever-increasing number of people other than yourself with significant interests and stakes in what you decide. They are more numerous than once thought: customers, employees, management, families, communities, government, suppliers, and investors. Stakeholders have varied and often clashing interests and concerns that affect your business in many ways. Increased stakeholders spell change: changes in the way business is done and the way decisions are made. You and I need to learn how to deal seriously with these new and varied stakeholders. They are a key ingredient in better decision making.

Second is a break with the past prompted by a changing world and marketplace. Your organizational issues, problems, and challenges traditionally were considered purely *business* issues, problems, and challenges, calling for purely business solutions. In the past few years, there has been a subtle, generally positive, but uncomfortable shift in public thinking. Issues, problems, and challenges are now increasingly viewed *ethically* as well, calling for both business and moral solutions.

As I watch, hear, and train organizational people like you across the United States, I see that there is an important unmet need in the marketplace. What's needed is a clear, practical decision-making process that enables you to decide and act from your own business and ethical values, as well as seriously consider what your concerned stakeholders value.

There is a lot of talk and emotion surrounding business ethics these days. Some people have graphically described the horrors of bad business and ethical decisions. Judgments and accusations have been leveled—most of the time without positive, concrete suggestions for change. Judging and accusing are not my purpose in this book.

There is another way toward change. Amid all the talk, emotion, and accusation, I have yet to hear of a decision-making process that joins ethics and business. I think you need one. I think you will use one well. The purpose of this book is to propose a new decision-making process that merges ethical values and business principles in a usable, practical, and positive way.

*A Rock and a Hard Place* is not a book of ready-made answers to organizational dilemmas. I am neither a business nor an ethics guru, nor do I want to be. I have deliberately not given my own answers to examples and cases in order to intrigue you into fashioning your own solutions.

The book is a guide or road map leading you to ask the right questions on the way to problem and dilemma solutions. And it will draw out your personal and organizational values and principles to help you make your own best choices.

So what's in it for you? Your decisions will be more effective, responsible, and therefore defensible. In today's business world and climate, such decisions are far more than a wishful ideal; they are a challenging and exciting necessity.

The structure and flow of the book will gradually prepare you to understand and use the three-step decison-making process. Learning, using, and doing are the practical goals. Each chapter builds on those preceding it. Each expands the theme of value-based decision making by presenting you with needed ideas and guidelines, illustrated with real-world examples and cases. Each chapter helps you personalize the material through short exercises focused on your work situation.

Chapter 1 again states the point of the book: value-based decision making as a necessary skill for facing the business and ethical issues of successful organizational life today. It then poses some decision-making ideals to be amplified as the book progresses.

Chapter 2 defines values and principles used in making choices and describes how you personally develop your own. It emphasizes the social and psychological experiences that helped form the value system you use in making personal decisons every day.

Chapter 3 takes you into the world of work, where organizational values, principles, and norms also drive decisions for action. The chapter gives examples of values and principles in existing organizations, showing how their stated values and principles mold unique identities, make these organizations different, and are intended to guide their decision making.

In Chapter 4, I discuss stakeholders and their value-based interests, which often conflict with those of others, including your own. Clashing interests give rise to organizational and personal issues and dilemmas, which are the business and ethical realities you must face.

Chapter 5 focuses on the role of ethics. There is a need for a new definition of ethics that is more useful, practical, and applicable to your needs. I present my own definition, which describes ethics as a necessary organizational skill for creating fitting, possible solutions to your business dilemmas.

The Universal General Moral Principles are the key link in ethical decision making, uniting business principles and options for action with a moral viewpoint. Chapter 6 outlines the traditional but little-discussed General Principles that I call the "Magnificent Seven."

The material in Chapter 7 breaks new ground for you as an architect of choices. It first shows the importance of ranking or prioritizing business options for action and the General Moral Principles they represent—a vital step in value-based decision making. Second, the chapter describes a new system, a moral attitude, for ranking business options and their General Moral Principles; this system hinges on the concept of responsibility. The new system is more responsive to the business and moral complexity you face in today's marketplace.

At this point, you are ready for the three-step decision-making process itself, presented in Chapter 8. It pulls together everything previously discussed into three decison-making steps: examining the situation, establishing the dilemma, and evaluating the options. The three steps are outlined, explained, and applied to a common, real-life case. You are then urged to choose your own dilemma and apply the process for the first time.

*A Rock and a Hard Place* would not be complete without an examination of the organizational dilemmas confronted in today's global marketplace. Cultural, ethical, and business differences among countries are noted in Chapter 9. More importantly, changes in your thinking and initiatives are proposed within the context of value-based decision making, responsibility, and the exciting but challenging opportunities outside the United States.

Ethics systems found in organizations are the focus of the last segment, Chapter 10. Choices driven by principles are not made in a vacuum. The three-step process needs to be surrounded by organizational systems that empower, support, and reward its use. This final chapter looks at a number of systems, some of which can be helpful in your own business situation.

What will be the payoff to you in learning and using this decision-making process? The benefit to you and your organization will be better decisions: choices that will be more effective, more responsible, and importantly, more justifiable. You will make your decision making more effective by combining unified moral and business principles for action in one process. You will seriously consider your own valid self-interest as well as the interests of key stakeholders, and so you will bring an enhanced attitude of responsibility to your efforts. Your decisions will be more defensible and justifiable, because moral and business reasons for action, taken together, generate a powerful argument to others.

I invite you to read on. The experience offers you new, usable ideas for your work situation. *A Rock and a Hard Place* is challenging and perhaps even controversial at times. Most of all, this book will help you become a better and more successful decision maker.

# Acknowledgments

I am grateful to the hundreds of organizational people with whom I have worked through the years. While I trained them, they taught me much about management, sales, organizational behavior, and human relations. Among them, I remember especially the hundreds of managers and salespeople around the United States who talked about their business dreams, efforts, and problems while I was an instructor for Wilson Learning Corporation.

How does one acknowledge, much less thank, the great thinkers and teachers of the past and present? During all the years I have studied and thought about philosophy, psychology, and various arts and skills, I have "lived" with great minds. I find that some of what they have taught me is reflected in this book. Aristotle, Thomas Aquinas, John Stuart Mill, Erich Fromm, Abraham Maslow, Carl Rogers, and Hans Selye, M.D., are but a few who have formed my thinking and enriched me.

While I was writing the book, several current philosophers, ethicists, and teachers helped me with current ideas and the formal discipline of ethics: Dr. Larry Goodwin, Dr. Bill Swenson, then director Doug Wallace, and the faculty of the Center for Ethics, Responsibilities and Values at The College of St. Catherine. I thank Larry, especially, for his interest, support, and help with the General Moral Principles and Bill for his ideas on responsibility. My gratitude also to the other thinkers, writers, teachers, and businesspeople quoted in the book.

I am grateful to Barbara Hauser, an international corporate attorney, who contributed much data to the chapter on decision making in the global arena. I also thank the many corporate people who furnished written and spoken information for my efforts.

Gratitude goes also to my AMACOM Books editor, Andrea Pedolsky, for her "tough-love" efforts and excellent editing ideas, which have been both necessary and helpful.

For patiently helping me solve the infinite mysteries of the PC, word processing, and manuscript preparation, I thank Steve Rosenbaum and Ann and Marc Lueck.

Finally, I most gratefully acknowledge the love and support of two cherished women in my life, Julie Parchman and my sister, Ann Hodgson.

"What matters most, however, is
where we stand as individual
managers and how we behave when faced
with decisions which require us to combine
ethical and commercial judgments."
—Sir Adrian Cadbury, chairman, Cadbury
Schweppes, p.l.c.

"This is the kind of ethical thing
you get into. It's not black; it's not white.
You're not responsible legally;
but you are responsible. The question is,
what are you responsible for?"
—Frank McGraw, purchasing manager

"We are made for cooperation."
—Marcus Aurelius

# A
# ROCK
# AND
# A
# HARD
# PLACE

# 1

# Life as a Decision Maker

## Making Choices Better, Not Perfect

Suppose you are the human resources director of a company that manufactures recreational vehicles, located in a small to medium-size town. Orders run in peaks and valleys. Last year, in response to a sudden large order, ninety people were hired and then let go thirty days later upon completion of the project. The community was angry and vocal, and company employees threatened to call in union organizers. At the time, you informally recommended that when a sudden, large order came in again, thirty-five people be hired and told they would have work for at least six months. Line managers vehemently shot down your idea, saying that the shortest delivery time line had to be kept or the company would risk losing contracts. They also felt there was no reason or obligation to tell new hires about the length of their employment. Last week, upper management asked managers to submit official recommendations for a production plan when such a scenario arose. What will you do?

Your initial thinking might go this way: "What's the current climate of thought and feeling around here about the problem? I have a decision to make, but what do I think about the situation—where am I coming from? How do I make my decision, and what will it be?" These questions, which you might ask about this real-life case, summarize the subject, content, purpose, and ideals of this book.

# The Subject

Personal and organizational decision making is the general subject of this book. More precisely, you, as a decision maker in
your own business or as a member of an organization, are the
subject.

But you don't make decisions in a void today. I remember
when, not long ago, managers said you ran a business with
"know-how." In the world in which we live, know-how changes
every day. Now you run a business and make decisions by
"learn-how."

And things don't seem as certain as they once did, either.
Many situations you face are complicated, difficult, and very
ambiguous. The people involved, the amount of money, the
ramifications, and the pressure to have the right answer are
immense. It's important to accept the climate in which you and
I make choices now. It used to be black or white. Today, it is no
longer black or white—we live in a "gray zone," where many of
the problems, challenges, and choices are tough ones. The case
of you as human resources director is a tough one. If it seems
simple to you, look at it again; consider all the interests involved
and the ramifications of the options you have to recommend.

But hard choices don't necessarily dictate bad judgments—
just the probability of nonperfect decisions in an imperfect
world. There are few perfect decisions made—by anyone—but
yours can be better if you "know where you're coming from."

Actually, you exercise a very personal decision-making
process. All your choices flow from and are driven by the values
and principles you hold about the situation you're facing. That's
"where you're coming from." You do more than just make
decisions; you make value-based decisions. The recommendations you give to upper management in the case just described
will come from certain values and principles that you hold about
production, hiring, and firing. And the process you will go
through is aimed at more than just thinking about an answer;
your decision will be about doing something—taking action. So
the subject of this book is values, principles, options, and
choices for action: your value-based decision making in the gray
zone of business and organizational life.

# The Purpose

My purpose in writing this book is twofold. First, you want your value-based decision making to be better; you want to keep improving. This book can help you a great deal with making better choices. Second, I present a concrete, practical way to make better decisions: a three-step process for value-based decision making that merges the main elements necessary for an effective, consistent, responsible, and defensible choice of action.

Recent business history has produced a litany of problems, mistakes, and even tragedies resulting from poor and sometimes horrendously bad decisions. You could recite them as well as I. Well-made choices of action and their good results are far less often recorded. Despite the history, immense and exciting opportunities for business are opening up all over the world. The problems, challenges, and opportunities of the 1990s should serve to intensify your attempts at better, more productive decisions.

As if to spur you on (though that may not be the direct intention), the media and the public have lots to say to you and organizations. From an ethical rather than a technical business viewpoint, books, articles, film, and TV proclaim that you and organizations *should* act more responsibly and with more integrity. Very little is offered anywhere on *how you can* act responsibly and with more integrity while still doing business successfully. I'm offering you a business and ethics process to do just that.

It's clear that the public is "ethics" conscious and quick to label organizations unethical and immoral. Some are; many, even most, are not. No one could know for certain without a recent history of business balanced with good news as well as bad. However, I do know with certainty that problems are often the result of poor personal and organizational decisions. The problems themselves, not just the media and public, spotlight the importance of the ethical factor, as well as the business factor, in decision making today.

But I'm convinced your challenges are not really that simple. Very often, the problems are not a question of bad intentions and evil actions. They are precisely a question of good business intent accompanied by an unsure grasp and application of ethics. Such problems represent a lack of knowing how to make business decisions that also have important and inseparable *moral* implications. It's a question of realizing that business factors and ethical factors go hand in hand; one factor cannot be part of decision making without the other. When business and ethical values are not considered together, bad decisions can be made and serious problems, even tragedies, result.

> "Because our values are clear, we believe it's easier for our people, from top to bottom, to make the right decisions about how this company should operate. . . . In a relationship built on trust, we must have our people work within an ethical framework."
>
> —Harvey Golub, chairman,
> IDS Financial Services, Inc.,
> and president, American Express

I suggest that you give far more attention to the values and principles—both business and ethical—that you hold, as these are behind the decisions you must and do make. Common sense and success in the gray zone demand it; your capabilities and resources, if tapped, are adequate for it; *A Rock and a Hard Place* is a guide for you to achieve it.

## Choice-Making Ideals

Certain decision-making ideals represent important goals for you. I mention them here both to set an agenda for what is to come in this book and to capture your attention and interest. The ideals, and the arguments for them, are developed throughout the book.

1. Almost every personal and organizational issue you face consists of both business and ethical factors. Admitting and accepting that fact will help you be a better decision maker.

2. Solving business/ethical issues and challenges is your work responsibility. It is not just the work of a few other top decision makers.
3. Decisions in organizations should be driven, as far as possible, by individuals with shared values—business principles and ethical principles held in common. This is value-based decision making.
4. Value-based decision making demands not only business skills, but also basic ethics skills. It implies that you know and use some sort of process that consciously merges the business and ethical factors inherent in most situations.
5. Decisions anchored in both business and moral values can produce solutions that, while not perfect, will be better—more effective, responsible, and defensible.

## The Challenge of Value-Based Decision Making

Any decision maker in the business world today who does not have basic ethics skills as well as business skills is in danger of being called professionally illiterate. That's the challenge of value-based decision making today. You can be better at making value-based choices. When you are, you and your organization will fulfill your professional purpose more successfully. This book aids you in meeting that challenge.

# 2

# Personal Ground Rules for Action

## How You Develop Values and Principles

Daily life is composed of numerous activities, and each action flows from a decision you make. That decision is driven by values you hold; the action reflects what you value. Whenever you decide to act, you're checking in with your own system of values—your "ground rules." In short, you constantly make value-based decisions for action.

We'll consider value-based decision making in a wider context—within organizations—later. First, let's examine your own personal values and principles, your own "ground rules" for action. What, exactly, are values and their working principles? What do they look like? Where did you get them? How are they key to decision making?

## What Are Values?

Values are what's worthwhile, or important, to you. Videotape "Wheel of Fortune" some weekday and watch contestants choose prizes based on what they value. Go to an auto dealership on a Saturday morning and watch a family purchase a car based on a set of values contained in price, color, payment terms, hearsay, and headroom. Watch your children laugh, pout, or cry based on how they value what you said. Or listen to a world leader state his or her country's position in the United Nations based on values of need, leadership, resources, or security.

*Values are ideas, qualities, or opinions you feel have worth*—like one game show prize over another, or a red minibus versus a black sedan, or "Let's eat" versus "Go make your bed." It's evident that some values center on things you want to have, and not just lofty things either. They can be anything.

Values can also center on what you want to do, like rest, work, vacation, or raise a family. Others focus on what you want to be: for instance, being successful, honest, educated, or a leader.

You have thousands of values—ideas, qualities, opinions that are important and desirable to you. Throughout your life, you have consciously or unconsciously heard, considered, and accepted a long list of personal values that make up your own value system. You've also rejected many ideas, qualities, or opinions as of no value. Hundreds of times a day, you make decisions for action checked against your values. Sometimes decisions are made in total awareness of your value system, as with buying a red minibus; sometimes the decisions appear to be automatic, as with locking the house door because you value safety. No matter what the decision, you check in with your values. Actions reflect what you value.

Mother Teresa cetainly has pronounced values. They are worthwhile and desirable to her, and many people believe, if asked, that they should be a standard for all of us. Ivan Boesky, the former arbitrageur, also has strong values, worthwhile and desirable to him, and with which many would agree. To him, they are as worthwhile and desirable as Mother Teresa's are to her. Abraham Lincoln and Adolf Hitler had strong values that they acted on to influence their countries and the world. Teddy Roosevelt, Margaret Sanger, Leonard Bernstein, Joseph Stalin, Pope John XXIII, Martin Luther King, Marilyn Monroe, Mohammed, and Michelangelo—all had strong values behind their history-making activities. They used their different but strongly held values to make choices of action in life.

# Values as Working Principles for Action

From childhood through adulthood, you have slowly, but not always consciously, developed a set of personal values. They can be directed to many things, like food, cars, or money. They can be about riding horses, baseball, art, quantum theory, or life after death. They can be qualities of human life, like happiness, justice, love, security, family, or fame. But values themselves are not only different and varied, but fairly abstract. To make decisions for actions based on your values, you develop a set of concrete operating principles that enable you to put values into action.

*A principle is a value of such worth to you that it becomes a standard you use to make decisions for action.* A principle is a practical, working guideline you use as a reason to have something, do something, or be something. For example, saying "A family is worthwhile" is stating a value. Saying "I will not work on Saturday so I can take my kids to the zoo" and "I favor time with my wife over playing golf" is stating operating principles based on a value—family. Working principles bring values into concrete form and drive specific actions and behaviors.

Concerning careers, for instance, some values are qualities, like leadership, education, financial success, fairness, or prestige. When those values are so important to you that they become working principles, or standards, you are then able to put them into action. For example:

| | |
|---|---|
| *Leadership:* | "I am next in line for vice-president." |
| *Education:* | "I am studying for my MBA." |
| *Financial success:* | "I am going to exceed my sales quota for the third straight year." |
| *Fairness:* | "I listen to the needs and problems of my work group." |
| *Prestige:* | "I have the lead article on business in my association journal." |

These activities are the result of values that have become working principles for action. Our values and principles are not always that clearly thought-out or stated, but they are there. What you do reflects and is driven by what you value.

## Your Values Are Uniquely Your Own

Your values and principles—your value system—are just that: *your* values and principles, not necessarily mine, not someone else's. You don't hold a value viewed as bad for you. A value you have accepted represents something good for you, at least at this time. It may not be a worthwhile value to someone else, but when you choose, for example, to eat a sandwich, drink a vodka tonic, become wealthy, adopt a child, write a report, rob a bank, or even commit suicide, you are performing an action driven by values and principles viewed as good for you now.

Certainly you reject values others may hold, and you change your own sometimes, but those you embrace and view as worthwhile now are uniquely yours and, more importantly, are the basis for what you want to have, do, or be. Very simply, your values and principles drive all your decisions and actions in life every minute of the day.

> "The poor do us the honor of allowing us to serve them."
> —Mother Teresa
>
> "Greed is a virtue and I don't apologize for it."
> —Ivan Boesky

## Where Did You Get Your Value System?

Working values and principles are developed from several sources. It's valuable to see how that development takes place, because it helps explain why you are the way you are and why you make certain decisions. The sources of your values and principles are your nature as a human being, the law, public opinion, religious authority, the community around you, conscience, and your own thinking and experience.

## *Doing What Comes Naturally*

Values are centered on your self-interest. They are part of your taking care of yourself first. That's how you survive, especially in the beginning. A baby needs and wants food, sleep, touching, pleasure, and freedom from pain. That babies are usually valued and adorable and hold future promise makes their lack of giving and their desire to take acceptable.

As a baby grows, though, the cooing, adorable self-interest no longer gives him carte blanche for all his behavior. And he begins to learn that his family and society emphasize certain values over others, rewarding positive behavior and punishing negative actions.

A child's evolving value system comes from several sources, not least of which is simply "doing what comes naturally." At an early age, a child learns that pleasurable feelings are better than painful ones. A full belly is better than an empty one—and she learns how to ask loudly for food. A warm home with a dry roof beats camping out in the rain anytime. The excitement of playing with matches can produce an "Ouch!" Natural inclinations—human drives for the basics of life, for survival itself—lead a child to value doing, having, being what she needs and wants. And she doesn't spend much time being aware of the needs and wants of others. Values and actions are largely self-centered.

That basic self-interest, or looking out for number one, is natural to each of us and is primary all our lives. It's not wrong; it's simply the way human beings are. Only later do you realize that you cannot survive and grow and prosper without other people. And these other people have their own self-interests at heart. You begin to learn that your independence must be balanced with interdependence, and you start to look at other ways to expand your value system.

## *It's the Law*

Values are acquired not only from the physical results of certain situations and actions but from their legal consequences. You've heard "It's the law" dozens of times, and people say it to emphasize that there must be some outside control to balance the competing self-interests of individuals.

Filching the candy bar in the store satisfies an aching sweet tooth, but is it worth the humiliation of being caught and dragged to the store manager in front of onlookers? And then the call to Mom or Dad at the office! You may value Snickers, but now you learn to weigh the candy bar against the value of not being punished. You learn more, too—that candy has a financial value to adults, and that actions, based on what you value, can adversely affect not only you but others.

So you learn to obey traffic signals. You weigh the legal and physical dangers of driving without a seat belt or of drinking one too many. Community and country have established laws to benefit and safeguard the majority of people. If you break the law, there will be consequences that the majority supports. You begin to sense that the rights and needs of others are also a part of your own survival and growth. Around that knowledge, certain values are formed, and certain decisions for living are made.

## Because "They" Said So!

Public opinion—in the form of ideas, requests, even demands— makes an impression on your value system. Besides written laws that permeate society, you are also subjected to equally strong unwritten laws or rules. They take many forms. Peers urge you to wear certain clothes, as do advertisers and TV programs. "Air Jordan" Nike shoes are proudly worn by teenagers as if part of a required school uniform. For teenage boys, football is cooler than croquet, and playing the trumpet in the school band carries more prestige than playing the tuba. Only recently have young women who play basketball been as cool as varsity cheerleaders. Parents lay down the verbal law at home about making beds and whom to date.

You often learn the unwritten rules not only by what you are told but by seeing how others act. And it is here that you are most likely to encounter the first contradictions. "Don't smoke," says a two-pack-a-day parent. On the playground, the school bully, not the principal, runs the fourth grade by force.

The sexually active boy is "macho," while the sexually active girl is "loose."

> "Do as I say, not as I do!"
> —A million
> anonymous parents

Even your community and country signal that there are unwritten rules and values. Working for a living is prized; importance and attention come from "success." People are to be treated equally, yet some seem to receive preferential treatment. Somehow it seems that skin color has a bearing on where one works and lives. American ideals, freedoms, and culture are to be protected and cherished, but you learn that other countries don't admire the United States (or its ideals) when they read of the homicide rate and the number of homeless families.

You see, hear, and learn about a variety of values from those around you. And two other facts are learned as well: One is that people have different values from yours, and the other is that values conflict with one another—your own within you, and your own with those of others. Remember when you were told you were too young to drink beer, but you wanted to so much that you did anyway? And how the kids at Calvary Lutheran down the block were against playing cards and dancing, while the gang at St. Agnes had to be against sex? And you thought, "Darn, why can't our church be against cards and dancing (which are easy to give up) instead of being against the best thing of all?"

## Because "He" Said So

Religious authority and teaching cannot be underestimated in the formation of basic values. For many people, personal values and principles can be traced directly to sacred books and their interpretation, liturgy, rituals, Sunday school, denominational K–12 schools, and preachers. This is particularly true in the areas of sexual customs, community relationships, marriage, child raising, the work ethic, and material goods.

Despite the separation of church and state, the written and unwritten laws of God as interpreted by authority dovetail frequently with secular ideas. The Golden Rule and the commandments against stealing are interpreted positively while one is sitting in the pew. On the street, they take on a more concrete meaning, emphasizing the smooth running of the neighborhood: You do not steal because you do not want others to steal from you. Therein lies anarchy.

Yet while religion is a strong influence on values, perhaps religious values are accepted without questioning far more than the other values mentioned. Take family moral decisions. I knew a man some years ago, the CEO of a large company, who each day made decisions alone that affected hundreds of people and millions of dollars. Yet he often called his parish priest in utter helplessness, trying to decide whether his kids should go to a movie with a C (condemned) rating on the Catholic Legion of Decency list. "He said so" is often *the* powerful force, not only on matters known only by faith, but often concerning ordinary value-based decisions in matters of daily living.

## We're in This Together

The need for survival and your own welfare formed many of your early values. Growing up, no matter which way you read it, develops an awareness that you are not just an individual with selfish needs. You are a person who must exist in a state of some harmony with a larger group, be it family, classroom, company, community, or nation—even the world—if you yourself are to survive and prosper. We are literally in this together. With this realization begins the formation of another set of values and principles around social responsibility: listening, helping, caring, sharing, and protecting.

## That "Still Small Voice" of Conscience

The voice of conscience reflects your value system. All your many values—ways of having, doing, and being—have been gradually and subtly absorbed by you and reinforced by family, friends, peers, neighbors, and colleagues. When confronted by a new situation, you automatically, without conscious thought, check in with principles that have become habits. This ability is one of the sources of your applied values and principles. Conscience is not a magic gift of genes or intelligence, but, it seems to me, an application to a given situation of values already chosen and principles already practiced.

This can simply mean "Am I gonna get away with it?" On a later and more mature level, you wonder if you feel "guilty" doing it. You are learning to refer to your value system, and to act on that system of worthy ideas and qualities. You are beginning to develop a habitual, stable, and coherent decision-making process. It may not reflect someone else's value system, but it does reflect your own.

> "Ultimately, an ethical choice comes down to a question: 'Can I live with that?' If not, don't do it."
> —Fred Friendly, former network executive

## Experience as Teacher

Throughout the search for a set of values and principles, you use the voice of experience. That voice is filtered through the ability to sense, remember, reason, and choose a course of action—our highest gifts as humans.

At first, your values were completely self-centered. Then you took authority at face value. Later you saw contradictions in the values around you, coupled with a need to live with others anyway.

You learn slowly that it is not a black or white world we live in: It is not just a matter of making value-based decisions that are simply right or wrong. Sometimes decisions assert your values over someone else's; sometimes they cause harm as well as good. Welcome to the real world of hard choices! I'll never forget the man who saw a young boy fall into a swollen, surging rapids. He thought quickly about his desire, even a command, to help. Then he thought about his responsibilities to his wife and three small children. And with a heavy heart, he had to let the boy go. Choices for action are sometimes deeply serious and, though right, tragic as well as good.

You learn that each of us has self-interest at heart, as well as responsibilities to others. These values frequently clash. You realize the world is indeed various shades of gray, not black or white. And to make fitting decisions that you can live with, you must read the shades. You are not always able to fall back simplistically on the Golden Rule, as good a guide as it is.

## Values Drive Decisions

Values and principles drive decisions in life. Every individual has a unique value system and different levels of commitment to those values. You gradually prioritize your values, knowing at some level which are the most important. That knowledge is important when principles come into conflict with each other and with those of other people around you, as they often will.

But it takes more than an awareness of your own value system and those of others to live, play, and work effectively. In the next chapter, we consider the organizational values and principles operating in the world of work. They, too, play an important part in your decision making.

## FINDING OUT ABOUT YOURSELF

I know you don't often spend time thinking about, much less writing down, your important values and working principles. It's hard for most of us to state them. But the clearer they are to you, the more effective they will be in your decision making. What are some of your major values and principles? Here is a helpful and enlightening exercise; try it. There are no correct answers, just values important to you.

1. Who is the best mentor, leader, teacher, supervisor, manager, or helper you've had? Why was that person best for you?

_____

_____

_____

_____

2. Think of two experiences in which you were going on all cylinders, at peak performance, at full potential.

_____

_____

3. List three things so important to you that without them your life would have little meaning.

_____

_____

_____

4. List a few values—ideas, opinions, qualities—that you consider worthwhile.

_____

_____

_____

_____

5. Choose ten of the following values that best describe your thinking:

   • Sense of accomplishment
   • Paying my own way
   • Adventure/risk/excitement
   • Being frank and genuinely myself
   • Personal independence and making my own choices
   • Service to others
   • Being good at something that's important to me
   • Having influence and authority
   • Having meaning to my life and/or religious belief
   • Physical health

- Emotional health
- Meaningful employment
- Caring for others, giving and receiving love
- Enjoyment/pleasure/fun
- Satisfying living situation
- Being recognized for having knowledge in a particular area
- Security in life and work
- Continuing to develop as a person

6. Now list the five major values you would choose from your list of ten, and add others important to you that were not included in the list.

_____

_____

_____

_____

_____

7. List four values you see operating in people around you at work or in your organization.

_____

_____

_____

_____

8. Take five of your top values and write them in terms of working principles. For example, the value "security in life and work" could have the working principle "I earn and will continue to earn the money it takes to be economically secure."

_____

_____

_____

_____

_____

_____

_____

_____

_____

_____

# 3

# What They Mean, and What They *Really* Mean

## The Values, Principles, and Norms of an Organization

In a personal and social setting, you check in with your own value system—your working principles—when deciding to act. Perhaps you own your own organization, but, more than likely, you work for an organization. Either way, you are called upon to make decisions for action in the name of that organization. It, like you, has principles that drive decision making. Your organizational decisions, then, flow from the values and principles of that organization as well as your own. In a real sense, the organization's working principles become yours—and that's important as you actually make choices for action.

In preparation for the value-based decision-making process presented in Chapter 8, I want you simply to experience selected examples of organizational working values and principles. They are not presented as good or bad, successful or not, in decision making. But they are what these companies have and use. I want you to see what they look like, how they sound, how they have a flavor or nuance peculiar to that company. I want you to sense how working values and principles help define what the organization is, how it is different from others, and how it intends to make a difference in the marketplace. Most organizations realize how important stating, adopting, and using their working principles is to their decision making. I intend to help you feel the same about your organization and your decisions. Those values, principles, and norms determine what you mean and what you *really* mean.

# What Are Organizational Principles?

Every organization has a set of values—in the form of working principles—that are reflected in their decisions. *Organizational principles, like personal principles, are values—ideas, qualities, or opinions—that an organization feels have worth and are desirable, and that have become standards by which it, and you, make decisions.* They have been formulated, considered, shaped, clarified, articulated, explained, and applied more or less clearly, but they are present in one form or another.

Organizational principles are ground rules that govern "the way business is done around here." Whether written or unwritten, spoken or unspoken, officially approved or not, they guide the complex organizational decison-making process. Unlike you personally, organizations involve anywhere from several to thousands of people in decision-making roles—from the board of directors, through top executives, managers, supervisors, and team leaders, all the way to support staff and other employees.

## Shared Values

Organizations intend that, as far as possible, their ground rules be "shared values"—principles that are known, accepted, and used by all members. Shared values have an important purpose: to attain the mission, goals, and objectives of the organization with unity, consistency, and effectiveness. Many organizations spend considerable time, energy, and money to create a climate in which a common set of ground rules are known, agreed upon, and applied in daily work activities. And that's true whether it's a large company like McDonnell Douglas or a small one like Minnesota Seed Capital, Inc., a small venture capital company.

The attainment of this climate—aligning principles and work decisions in order to act in unity—is far from uniform, complete, or perfect in all organizations. One estimate is that 90 percent of managers know their organizations have a guiding set of principles, while 50 percent or fewer have received a copy of them, and about 5 percent of managers connect their day-to-day work with the guiding principles.[1] And that's just managers. However, I think that estimate reflects a lack of full execution, not of desire. The goal of truly shared ground rules—from vision to practical use by all—is not easily attained.

Some notable companies do better than that. *Corporate Ethics: A Prime Business Asset* (1988), a report on policy and practice in company conduct by The Business Roundtable, found that Boeing, Champion International, Chemical Bank, General Mills, McDonnell Douglas, Norton, Xerox, and many others have successfully gone through a long and extensive process of values formulation and application.[2] Numerous other organizations, large and small, strive to align their ground rules with their decision making.

Shared organizational principles alone do not guarantee effective, consistent, and successful decisions, but they are key in the effort to become more effective, consistent, and successful. A mission statement, written company policies, codes of ethics, and a manual of policies and procedures alone—written by top executives and the legal department, and presented at a half-hour meeting of all employees—are not going to ensure compliance or use in the daily routine of business. Members of the organization must make the working principles their own. One company calls that needed commitment an employee "way of life."

Some organizations feel the necessity of establishing working principles from the top down, while others involve some or all of their employees. Either way, eventually, there must be a buy-in by members of the organization if the established values and principles are to be used effectively in decision making. Employees will not simply do what they are told to do; they must be allowed and urged to willingly make organizational principles part of what *they* value, personally. Then they can be expected and required to apply them in work situations.

I heard a story some years ago that illustrates the power of both shared values and buy-in of members in an organizational setting. A Denver TV station lost a key antenna in the foothills outside of town during the night in a fierce blizzard. One of the broadcast technicians, acting out "shared responsibility" (an emphasized principle at the station), rented a pickup, grabbed the necessary equipment, put on his parka, stuffed a manual into his pocket, drove through the drifts, and spent two hours repairing the antenna. He put the station back on the air. He didn't call his supervisor or the maintenance director or the operations vice-president—he just took care of it.

> "Organizations that do not have a heritage of mutually accepted, shared values tend to become unhinged during stress, with each individual bailing out for himself. . . . In a complex corporate situation, the individual requires and deserves the support of the group. If people cannot find such support from their organization, they don't know how to act."
>
> —Bowen H. McCoy, president,
> Morgan Stanley Realty, Inc.

## An Identity

Organizational principles also define identity. They give an organization a "look," a personality, a uniqueness. They tell employees and the public who the organization is, what it does, how it makes a difference, and how it does business. Organizational principles should be used for more than PR. They are the core of an organization's culture—its heritage—and with them individuals can make decisions that reflect the core culture.

Decision making is driven by principles more than by products and services. AT&T, MCI, and Sprint are all companies dealing in telecommunications, but their working principles, their particular identity and heritage, and therefore their decisions, are not uniformly alike. You sense it not only in their ads, but even more so in their marketing: one traditional and trusted, one aggressive and claiming to be cheaper, one boasting quality of hearing tone.

The Chicago Bears, Denver Broncos, and Los Angeles Raiders all play professional football, but they don't have the same guiding organizational principles—the heritage from which decisions are made. Just watch how differently coaches Mike Ditka and Dan Reeves and Raiders owner Al Davis make organizational and field decisions.

## Organizations Form Their Own Principles

Organizational values and principles are formed, chosen, adopted, and promulgated—not discovered. They are sometimes stated in the words and actions of the organization's founder. They are contained in the words of top executives, mission and purpose statements, official statements of policy, codes of ethics, and policy and procedure manuals. Over a period of time, you can see them in action by observing the everyday routine of an organization's activity: you can hear them by listening to the stories and myths that are part of the company culture. Look at some examples of organizational values and principles.

### *In Words*

In the early days of an organization, values and principles often spring from the words of founders themselves or those close to them. Robert Wood Johnson, son of the founder of Johnson & Johnson, wrote the following when promoting an employee to a sales management position in the early 1890s: "What we want is reliability and close attention to details . . . someone who, in taking charge, does not make men work more than he performs."[3]

Fashion retailer Cedric A. Kirchner, founder and owner of Cedrics Enterprises, Inc., is said to often refer to the three Cedrics Cs: character, credibility, and confidence.

Guiding principles are often formed by top executives. Sir Adrian Cadbury, chairman of Schweppes PLC, wrote that one of the most common ethical issues companies face is how far to go in buying business.

What payments are legitimate for companies to make to win orders and, the reverse side of that coin, when do gifts to employees become bribes? I use two rules

of thumb. . . . Is the payment on the face of the
invoice? Would it embarrass the recipient to have the
gift mentioned in the company newspaper?[4]

Those kinds of written values give birth and meaning to strong
organizational principles.

Larry Wilson, founder of Wilson Learning Corporation—
an international management, sales, and customer service training company—used to say that "WLC helps organizations be all
they can be and have fun doing it." In earlier days, WLC's
clients saw that the company lived out those values in its
decisions and in its courses.

### In Mission and Purpose Statements

Organizational values and principles are found in mission or
purpose statements that answer the questions "Why are we
here?" and "How do we make a difference?" Purpose statements take many forms and lengths. Here are just a few examples from various organizations and individuals. Each one is
distinctly different, yet each clearly states the working principles:

> Our Mission: we are in business to please our
> customers. By giving them the value they seek in
> terms of quality merchandise that is both fashion-right
> and competitively priced.
>
> By having the most wanted merchandise in
> stock—in depth—in our stores.
>
> By giving them a total shopping experience that
> meets their expectations for service, convenience, en-
> vironment and ethical standards.
>
> Everything we do—throughout our organiza-
> tion—should support and enhance the accomplish-
> ment of this mission.[5]

Other examples from individuals and organizations:

> "I translate information into knowledge through
> my own experience and communicate this for others
> to grow and develop."

"I am doing good, helping others, while enjoying success for all to see. I am assisting other people to be free and healed."

"Our Charter/Mission: to be a quality communications company, serving the needs of the information marketplace while pursuing selective opportunities that capitalize on the strength of our resources; also to increase the value of shareholders' investment while maintaining fair treatment of employees and fulfilling corporate citizenship responsibilities."

"We provide great food served quickly by attractive, friendly people in a warm, fun atmosphere."

## What Do Working Values and Principles Look Like?

Here are a few examples of organizational values not yet in the form of principles. Some are "quality of work" values: control, teamwork, communication, measurement, professionalism, organizational economy, and environment. Others are "quality of life" values: individual respect, personal challenge, growth, enthusiasm, ethics, work/life balance, and rewards. "Quality of management" values include business and organizational understanding, relating job to society, trust, recognition, relating past, present, and future, leadership, and spirit.

A good way to understand working values and principles is to look at what organizations in various industries and sizes have written in forming their working principles. Not surprisingly, these principles are written in a variety of styles—some couched in concise, legal language, some in business activity jargon, others in informal, even folksy terms. We can see that even the language and style in themselves are an indication of certain shared values. Here are a few examples, excerpted from publications of the organizations noted. I want you to sense both the values chosen and the nuances peculiar to the industries and companies.

### By the Book

Chemical Bank is one of the largest U.S. banks, with thirty thousand employees. It shouldn't surprise us, then, to learn that

Chemical's *Code of Ethics* is highly detailed, and the language quite formally legal. After all, banking was—and perhaps will be again—a highly regulated industry, dealing with corporations' and individuals' money. That's why we find that responsibility is the key value stressed by the bank. Its working principles include the constant maintenance of confidentiality, since the reputation of the corporation depends on it. In addition, "There is honesty and candor in our activities, including observance of the spirit as well as the letter of the law."

Other values and principles include:

> A sense of fairness toward all who have a stake in the bank, avoidance of conflicts between personal interests and the interests of the Corporation, or even the appearance of such conflicts, . . . maintenance of our reputation and avoidance of activities which might reflect adversely on the Corporation; integrity in dealing with our assets. . . . Overall, Chemical believes that trust is the cornerstone of the financial services business.[6]

Quite formal, this. But then it's a bank, and we wouldn't want our banker joking around with our money—especially these days.

### Fun, Risk, and Guest Obsession

Practically on the other end of the formality spectrum is T.G.I. Friday's, which operates over 140 casual theme restaurants nationally and employs more than fifteen thousand people. It, too, has a written list of values contained in its managers' training manual, which puts integrity first. The chain's working principle: "To live by the highest level of integrity and ethics— without this there is no trust or credibility."

Wait a minute—what's so informal about that? After integrity, T.G.I. Friday's next lists as a value: "Have fun!" The restaurant wants its staff to apply this to all aspects of their lives. The manual insists that employees balance their priorities: "Your health comes first—without it you have nothing; your family comes second; T.G.I. Friday's comes third. Recognize and nurture the first two so that you can take care of the third."

The company's manual even encourages employees to take risks. "Recognize the freedom to make mistakes; progress involves risk; growth, through well-managed failure, is acceptable."

A people-centered company? Yes, but that's what you would expect—and too often don't get—in a restaurant chain. T.G.I. Friday's knows that it's in the business of serving people—and serving them more than a hamburger. The company calls it "guest obsession." One example from its manual illustrates this obsession, as well as the chain's sense of humor: It refers to the movie *Five Easy Pieces,* where Jack Nicholson's character asks for a side order of whole wheat toast in a diner. The waitress says they don't serve side orders of whole wheat toast. Nicholson's character notices on the menu that the chicken salad sandwich comes on whole wheat bread. The annoyed waitress points to a sign that reads, NO SUBSTITUTIONS and WE RESERVE THE RIGHT TO REFUSE SERVICE TO ANYONE. Thoroughly irritated at this point, Nicholson's character orders a chicken salad sandwich on whole wheat toast, but he tells the waitress to hold the mayo, the lettuce, and the chicken salad— just to bring him the whole wheat toast. Equally sarcastically, she asks where she should hold the chicken salad. Nicholson responds, "Between your knees." The manual's moral: "You are responsible for training your employees that any guest request within reason will be honored."[7]

## Doing Well by Doing Good

The Dayton Hudson Corporation is a retail business made up of a family of companies. Yet serving society is the corporation's stated overriding value. Its working principles read:

> The business of business is serving society, not just making money—profit is the means and measure of our service, but not an end in itself; we serve four major publics: customers, employees, shareholders, communities; our personal and financial involvement in community giving, community development and

government affairs help us manage our business
better.

Considering Dayton Hudson's growth and reputation, its values
have helped manage its business quite well. And there are scores
of communities that have benefited from its growth.

Regarding its people, the corporation insists "on competitive compensation, performance appraisal, training and development, and [we] prefer to hire from within; we want our people
at all levels to have the opportunity for stable, long-term careers;
we seek a work atmosphere that encourages employee initiative
and input and which fosters trust and creativity; we're far from
perfect, and we aim to get better."[8]

The corporation's values and principles statements cover
all of its activities, from positioning the business to managing,
governing, operating, and merchandising. Throughout, the company describes itself in clear, concrete, direct, and forceful
business terms, avoiding both legalese and abstraction. Almost
without exception, two other themes or values run through each
of the areas described: customer satisfaction (the company's
hassle-free, no-argument return policy is legendary) and responsibility—to its customers, employees, and communities.

## A Whisk Broom in Your Hip Pocket

Another retailer, although hardly as large as Dayton Hudson, is
Cedrics Enterprises, Inc., a privately owned, high-fashion ap-
parel store. Its stated main value is quality, and its working
principles include offering excellent clothing and developing a
staff that is the best in high-fashion merchandising.

Cedrics stresses service, the kind of service that we remember from several decades ago when we visited the local gas
station. The attendant not only filled up the tank and did the
windows, but also cleaned out the floors of the car with a whisk
broom so the customer would come back. Cedric Kirchner,
founder and owner, demands that his staff carry a "whisk
broom" of great service in their back pockets.

Other values, which flow from service, are necessary for
trust: the trust of a customer in a salesperson, and the trust of
staff in the owner. Such values include honesty and character:

"If the suit doesn't make the customer look good, or doesn't fit, and you can't tell them honestly that it does, don't sell it," says Kirchner. And finally, outstanding service requires a strong work ethic: "You gotta be fishin' when they're bitin' "—you've got to be there when the customers are there.[9]

Like many companies that are owned and run hands-on by the founder, Cedrics attempts to mirror in its actions the values and principles of an experienced, outspoken, high-risk entrepreneur, and the store reflects his ideas and presence.

## We Did It Our Way

Champion International Corporation, a paper products and building materials manufacturer, has also developed a comprehensive document that details its values. Called *The Champion Way Statement,* it sets forth a series of standards that formed part of the basis for major cultural changes in this large corporation—changes that involved cost reduction, greater productivity, participative management, quality improvement, and increased profits.

Champion stresses "leadership through profitable growth, requiring the active participation of all employees in increasing productivity, reducing costs, improving quality and strengthening customer service. This will benefit all to whom we are responsible—shareholders, customers, employees, communities and society at large."

In order to achieve these benefits and become an industry leader, Champion knew it had to develop and follow a series of working principles based on certain other values. In the document it stresses:

### Excellence

We want to be known for the excellence of our products, service and the integrity of our dealings; we want to be known as an excellent place to work. . . . We want to be known for our fair and thoughtful treatment of employees. . . . We believe in the individual worth of each employee and seek to foster personal development; through the individual actions of employees,

committed to excellence, long-term economic success
and leadership position will be ensured.

## Communities

We want to be known as a public-spirited corporation,
mindful of its need to assist . . . nonprofit, educational,
civic, cultural and social welfare organizations.

## Openness and Truth

We want to be known as an open, truthful company,
committed to the highest standards of business conduct in our relationships. . . . We are unequivocal in
our support of the laws of the land and acts of questionable legality will not be tolerated.

## Environment

We want to be known as a company which strives to
conserve resources, reduce waste, use and dispose of
materials with scrupulous regard for safety and health
. . . [and comply] with the spirit and letter of all
environmental regulations.[10]

## The Value of Profit

Lest we forget, some companies simply want to make money.
Minnesota Seed Capital, Inc., a small, early-stage venture capital company, makes no bones that its main value is return on
investment. Its working principle is to "provide a superior rate
of return for our investors through long-term equity investments."[11] And that's a perfectly legitimate value. This is a
company that wants to become a significant player in investment
management.

## The Value of Individuals

Another company—a bit larger this time—says right up front
that its main value is trust and respect for individuals. Hewlett-
Packard, the computer and electronic measuring equipment

manufacturer, states that it is committed to giving its people the proper tools and support so that they can do their jobs well.

From this main idea flow all of HP's other values—and the company's growth. HP customers expect its products and services to be of the highest quality and to provide lasting value. Because of this expectation, all "HP people, but especially managers, must be leaders who generate enthusiasm and respond with extra effort; people should be looking for new and better ways to do their work."

While the company believes that a profit is the essential measure of corporate performance, there should be an "adherence to the highest standards of business ethics. . . . Anything less is totally unacceptable. . . ." Ethical conduct "cannot be assured by written HP policies and codes; it must be an integral part of the organization, a deeply ingrained tradition passed on from one generation of employees to another."[12]

In addition, Hewlett-Packard stresses teamwork, flexibility, and innovation. Hewlett-Packard's values statements reflect a large number of identified principles that have been reflected upon and honed for many years. Unlike many other organizations, HP has strong, integrated statements on the basic goodwill of employees, the importance of trust, and the necessity of innovation with cooperation.

## What We Believe

Even without the widely publicized Tylenol situation and solution, Johnson & Johnson's values and principles, both in writing and as part of the company culture, would be a striking example of the effectiveness and simplicity that can be attained by values put into action for decision making.

*Our Credo,* the code of behavior for the highly diversified international health care corporation, has been used, discussed, and shaped for more than forty years. This extremely powerful document is very different from most organizational statements and codes. It does not even mention the word *honesty.* Its simplicity of language and style belies the depth of its meaning and intent. *Our Credo* is tied by design and language into the regular concerns of doing business—from product choice to maintenance of property, taxes, research, compensation, and financial reserves. It speaks directly to the need for profit but, most unusually, puts forth in the form of a working principle that a fair return is obtained through ethical behavior. Uniquely, Johnson & Johnson's values and principles are seen as company "responsibilities," or relationships, to its stakeholder groups: customers, employees, communities in which the company is located, and stockholders.

The best way to experience this unique example of organizational values and principles is to read it in full.

## Our Credo

We believe our first responsibility is to the doctors, nurses and patients, to mothers and fathers, and all others who use our products and services. In meeting their needs everything we do must be of high quality. We must constantly strive to reduce our costs in order to maintain reasonable prices. Customers' orders must be serviced promptly and accurately. Our suppliers and distributors must have an equal opportunity to make a fair profit.

We are responsible to our employees, the men and women who work with us throughout the world. Everyone must be considered as an individual. We must respect their dignity and recognize their merit. They must have a sense of security in their jobs. Compensation must be fair and adequate, and working conditions clean, orderly and safe. We must be mindful of ways to help our employees fulfill their family responsibilities. Employees must feel free to make suggestions and complaints. There must be equal opportunity for employment, development and advancement for those qualified. We must provide competent management, and their actions must be just and ethical.

We are responsible to the communities in which we live and work and to the world community as well. We must be good citizens—support good works and charities and bear our fair share of taxes. We must encourage civic improvements and better health and education. We must maintain in good order the property we are privileged to use, protecting the environment and natural resources.

Our final responsibility is to our stockholders. Business must make a sound profit. We must experiment with new ideas. Research must be carried on, innovative programs developed and mistakes paid for. New equipment must be purchased, new facilities provided and new products launched. Reserves must be created to provide for adverse times. When we operate according to these principles, the stockholders should realize a fair return.[13]

---

"The law libraries are full of texts about codification of laws. As soon as you make a rule, people argue about it. What is so powerful about the Credo is that the document is so simple. You have to decide what is the right course in a specific instance."
—James E. Burke, former chairman, Johnson & Johnson

---

Clearly, many organizations intend that their decisions for action be driven by shared, written (or spoken) values and principles. These standards are meant to be applied by decision makers in particular situations and circumstances. Is there, then, a guarantee of effective, unified, consistent, and ethical decisions? No. Are these principles necessary and useful in moving in the right direction? Absolutely; otherwise, the many prominent and successful organizations I investigated wouldn't commit the time, energy, and funds to formulating and applying their principles.

## Norms: The Way Business Is *Really* Done Around Here

But there is another set of principles—called norms—that organizations and the individuals in them use in making decisions. Written principles let others know what the organization means; norms, largely unwritten and unofficial, often let others know what the organization *really* means.

*A norm is a working principle that is in some way accepted by all or part of an organization as a standard for decision making, but is not written or promulgated officially.* Norms are informal principles that organizations use to do, have, or be something. They are not found in mission statements, or in codes of ethics, or in policy and procedure manuals. But they are in use by various groups in the organizations.

In most organizations, there are many norms that are practical implementations of company policy and practice. They reinforce and apply stated values and principles, with which they are in agreement. But the bad news is that many norms are at variance with established values and principles. They are the subject of such comments as ''Yeah, well, this is what we're supposed to be doing, but here's what really goes on, and you better know that.'' Norms often reflect the ''Don't do as I say, do as I do'' mentality, which, of course, sends a contradictory message.

My emphasis is on the norms that work against the written and desired values and principles. Such norms represent a real danger to ethical decision making. Unwritten norms that supersede, undermine, trivialize, or ridicule the stated principles wreak havoc in organizations, because there is a double standard at work. Unwritten, negative norms confuse management, employees, and other stakeholders who don't know the actual rules of the game at any given moment.

Here are some stated principles followed by negative norms that I have personally experienced. You will undoubtedly recognize them. They are not presented cynically; rather, I intend to clearly differentiate the negative norms from the fully accepted values and principles of an organization. Certainly, not all of these norms are accepted or practiced by all organizations, but every organization has at least some of them. The questions you should be asking about them are ''What is their effect on my organization?'' and ''What should be done about them?''

| *Stated Working Principles* | *Unstated Norms* |
|---|---|
| We encourage employees to bring up ideas and complaints. | Never knock it unless you have a better idea. |
| Your personal life is your own. | If you're going to work for this company, you better own one of the cars we make. |
| A clean, professional appearance is all we ask. | If you want to get ahead, you better know where the nearest Brooks Brothers is. |
| If you are experiencing personal problems, we encourage you to seek appropriate help. | Never admit you have problems; it can kill your promotion or get you fired. |

Take responsibility for your mistakes so that we can all work together as a team to solve them.

Admitting mistakes is poor politics; it can get you canned.

We expect you to achieve your quota.

We expect you to reach your quota, no questions asked.

We deliver a top-quality product to our customers at a fair price.

Quality is cut if it really affects the bottom line.

All we ask is that you do your work.

Fake it till you make it.

We do not tolerate sexual harassment.

Just don't give him or her a court case.

All expenses must be legitimate and fully reported.

It's not padding, it's perks—and I've earned them.

Lack of productivity and skills will be handled in private by your manager, who will give you the needed coaching.

Don't expect much help, and if you goof up, be prepared for a public tongue-lashing.

The benefits of our success will be shared by all employees.

The higher-ups make ten times what we make, and *we* get the product out the door.

Sales personnel on the floor will do some merchandise ticket marking when needed.

Top producers never mark tickets, they just sell; we do the rest of the work.

No long-distance phone calls for personal reasons are permitted.

She makes five calls a week to relatives back East, and nothing happens.

Our new code of ethics is what we all stand for and will use for the conduct of daily business.

We went to a meeting, someone talked on the ethics code for half an hour, and we all had to sign a paper that we understood it and will follow it.

Men and women will be paid equally for comparable positions in our company.

Women still average 20 percent less than men in comparable positions.

The field sales force is urged to call the VP of marketing whenever they need special help.

Salespeople who make their quotas regularly have calls to the VP returned; salespeople who don't never get a return call.

More than ever before, people in good organizations today realize how important it is to "walk your talk." An essential ingredient in effective decision making is to model the ground rules. Let others, especially your subordinates, see you live out organizational principles. People adopt organizational values and principles if they see that others, especially those above them, have adopted and use those same ground rules.

But modeling principled behavior is largely unproductive if the most powerful force in decision making is a set of negative norms at variance with the official values and principles. For example, if confidentiality is a shared value, but company personnel records are not really confidential, then the norm is what determines decisions, not the official principle. When theft occurs, but no one will "rat" on the thief, then a norm is the principle at work. If equal facilities for all employees is the written policy, but some people have private parking spaces near the entrance, then the norm is what really runs things. In some companies, top managers are urged to use employee assistance services for their stress and alcohol problems. But the fact that a manager has used the service is soon known and employed as a weapon by his or her peers. Then a norm has the power, not a company principle. If school administrators are not to have "slush funds," but they do, then the negative norm powerfully discourages others from using the stated principles to make daily decisions. When "politics is the norm," then what happens to a stated principle of open, candid communication?

Unified, consistent, and effective decision making depends on the ability of all the stakeholders to depend on the same ground rules. Norms that are out of sync with the shared values and principles should be identified, rendered unrewarding, and eliminated to the extent possible. This is no small task, as anyone who has tried to do it knows. But effective decision making that purports to be fitting, responsible, and justifiable demands it.

I am under no illusion that an identified, discussed, written set of shared values guarantees that organizations will use them successfully, consistently, or even at all in decision making. Even successful organizations, including the ones mentioned, have at least two characteristics pertinent to this discussion: (1) They have made mistakes, sometimes serious mistakes, in their own decision making by not following their own stated values; and (2) it is easy to find someone who will say they simply don't or sometimes don't live up to their stated values.

But what is pertinent to all of us (to quote the Dayton Hudson Corporation) is that "we're far from perfect, and we aim to get better." What is clear, as we shall see in the next chapter, is that when the "crunch" of real organizational dilemmas comes, you had better be able to ask the right questions, have a set of principles to guide you, and be in a position to make the best possible choices for action.

## Finding Out About Yourself

If you are among the 90 percent who can't recite the official guiding principles of their organization, or not among the 5 percent who use them for day-to-day decision making, this exercise is for you. Try it, and if you have to, do a little research to find the answers.

1. Using the values and principles of companies quoted in this chapter as examples, name three written values your organization officially stands for.

   _____

   _____

   _____

   _____

2. Name some official, written working principles that concretize the values noted in question 1.

   _____

   _____

   _____

   _____

3. Do you use the accepted ground rules just noted to make

decisions in your work? If not, why do you think you haven't used them?

_____

_____

_____

_____

4. Using the norms quoted in this chapter as examples, name some unofficial negative norms that operate in your organization—that is, unwritten principles used on the job that represent "the way we *really* do business around here."

_____

_____

_____

_____

5. Are the norms you named at variance with your official, accepted ground rules? If so, what can you do about it?

_____

_____

_____

_____

# Notes

1. Estimate of Thomas L. Brown from his consulting work with organizations on vision and values, and as contributing editor of *Industry Week*, July 21, 1988, p. 3.
2. *Corporate Ethics: A Prime Business Asset*, The Business Roundtable, 1988.
3. Lawrence G. Foster, *Johnson & Johnson: A Company That Cares* (1986), p. 37.
4. Sir Adrian Cadbury, ''Ethical Managers Make Their Own Rules,''

*Harvard Business Review* (September/October 1987), p. 72. Copyright © 1987 by the President and Fellows of Harvard College; all rights reserved.

5. *Management Perspectives Executive Summary,* Dayton Hudson Corporation, 1989.
6. *Code of Ethics,* Chemical Banking Corporation, May 1989.
7. *Management Training Introduction,* T.G.I. Friday's, Inc., 1990.
8. *Management Perspectives Executive Summary,* Dayton Hudson Corporation, 1989.
9. From an interview with Cedric Kirchner, December 18, 1990.
10. *The Champion Way Statement: The Champion Way in Action,* Champion International Corporation, December 1988.
11. From an interview with Ray Allen, president, COO, and general partner, Minnesota Seed Capital, Inc., December 9, 1990.
12. *Corporate Objectives,* Hewlett-Packard, July 1989.
13. *Our Credo,* Johnson & Johnson, revised January 11, 1991.

# 4

# The Many Horns of a Dilemma

## When Interests Clash

Each day at work, you make many choices for action using your own values and principles, together with those of the organization you represent. Decisions are what get the job done.

Some of your decisions attempt to meet small needs and resolve small problems; some deal with larger issues and problems. All of them, in some way, involve people—what they want, how they act, how you want them to act. Do any of the following problems sound familiar?

- What do you do about patterns of purchasing from suppliers in a recessionary period?
- How can you bring controversial problems to supervisors when you may be open to career reprisals?
- How do you handle a chemically dependent employee who has been through treatment with no increase in productivity?
- Should you move your production facility to a location with a cheaper labor pool?
- How do you stop the loss of $10,000 worth of missing pencils, bond paper, correction fluid, nonbusiness copying, and personal long-distance phone calls a year?
- How do you replace two older, long-term employees who just can't do the job anymore?

- What do you do when an employee charges sexual harassment on the basis of looks alone?

One thing is sure. These and many other issues arise—some easy, some difficult—and they must be faced and resolved. In this chapter, you'll consider several key elements involved in your problem solving: the reality and importance of stakeholder interests; what dilemmas—the clash of stakeholder values—look like today; and, finally, why dilemmas are the stuff of your value-based decision making.

## When Values and Principles Collide

Your values and principles have been shaped, revised, and used over the years. While you have shared common problems with others, your values and principles, like your fingerprints and DNA, are unique to you. And so it is with every other person around you.

Organizations also have sets of values, working principles, and norms they bring to bear on problems in the workplace. Like you, each organization has its own unique value system.

With all of us—each person and organization—representing our own needs and interests, what happens? We can dream about the best of all possible worlds, where business decisions benefit everyone all the time. But we know that in reality there is an overriding collision of values and purposes. Call it human nature, call it business as is, call it healthy competition—the collision of values, principles, decisions, and actions is part and parcel of the real world.

When organizational and individual principles for action collide, you and I have to face certain issues and dilemmas. Dilemmas are tough calls, like those mentioned earlier in the chapter, that involve serious interests. And they often have ethical dimensions. Ethical dilemmas demand your special attention as a decision maker and call upon you to make appropriate decisions.

## Stakeholders' Interests

Values and principles represent what we hold as worthwhile and desirable—ideas, qualities, or things we want to do, have, or be.

If you value health, for example, you choose activities that foster your good health. What you value you are interested in. You have a "stake" in good health. Where decisions about health are concerned, you are a stakeholder. Say that you're about to manufacture a new aerobic exercise machine for home use. You are a stakeholder in the project; so is the supplier of the materials for the machine; so is the first customer. All of you have a meaningful interest or stake in the product.

*Stakeholders are people who have an interest in a situation and are affected by its solution.* Stakeholders "own" and represent their values; they need and want what they value. Most importantly, stakeholders will pursue and compete for their interests within a project setting. They make action decisions driven by their interests—they "stake out" their claim. If you want to know what someone really values, look first at his or her actions and then backtrack from the actions, through the decisions, to interests—the basic values. Actions reflect values.

## Stakeholders Today

In the ever-growing complexity of a shrinking world, the list of acknowledged stakeholders has grown considerably. No longer can an organization deal only with stockholders or investor partners, management, customers, and employees, in that order. Now, employees' families, suppliers, distributors, neighborhoods, communities, state and federal government, the country, and indeed the world have been added to the list. And the number and priority of interested parties changes with each business situation.

> "For corporations to say our only responsibility is to stockholders is to deny our place in the social ecosystem."
> —Jim Autry, president, the magazine group, Meredith Corporation

Take communities, for instance. The cities, towns, and neighborhoods in which an organization operates certainly have stakes in that organization. They rely on the organization's employees and the company's taxes to contribute to their obligations. In return, municipalities may offer service, tax breaks, or other incentives to ensure that the company remains and grows. We have watched this interplay between organizations and communities in the awarding of major sports franchises; we've seen it in the impact of proposed military cutbacks on local manufacturing plants and bases. We witness the rapid development of a rural area when an auto manufacturer announces a new plant and product—and the failure of shops and restaurants when a plant closes and unemployment rises in a small town. As a company prospers or weakens, so do its stakeholders—a whole area, a state, and possibly even segments of the national economy.

With today's global market atmosphere, in which changing forms of government and economic philosophy blur regional borders, significant chunks of the world become organizational stakeholders. In 1988, who foresaw that sudden changes in Eastern Europe would have consequences for the U.S. energy, defense, computer, food, and transportation industries? Or that the war in the Middle East would affect families, banks, manufacturers, and service companies?

Today there is a long list of issues, programs, and situations that symbolize stakeholder "interests": work conditions, leisure time, maternity/paternity leave, child care, education, career planning, outplacement, employee stock option plans, employee assistance programs, unions, affirmative action and equal employment opportunity, waste disposal, social activism, pressured legislatures, university research, the environment, government regulations, and financial services, to name only a few. Stakeholders themselves include sophisticated customers and clients, investigative journalists, neighborhood citizen groups, city councils, proposition-minded voters, suppliers with special clout, outside consultants, health providers, and stockholders—all the varied constituencies with a stake in the action demanding your consideration.

## Potential for Conflict

Uniqueness of interests—personal and organizational—in the workplace opens the door to conflict among stakeholders.

Each of us is familiar with the conflict among our own values on the private level. Will you work in your own business, or for a corporation? Do you want children, or will you keep yourself free for a career? Do you really like this kind of work? Can you split time between home and job? We also witness and experience the conflict of interests among family members, friends, and neighbors—and conflicts over finances, religion, politics, and relationships.

But in the organizational environment, the potential for conflict of values and stakes is multiplied. Your own stakes are thrown into a melee of resource allocation, power, departmental interests, career advancement, mandated goals and objectives, and just plain corporate politics and norms. You find yourself conflicting with other stakeholders in the ordinary give-and-take of work. Positively speaking, these clashes of values and stakes can lead to new ideas, better systems, better marketing strategies, new personnel policies, or higher production figures. But not always.

### Personal/Organizational Conflicts

You may find yourself in serious clashes with the stated values and principles of your organization at a time when decisions for action have to be made. Issues that may spark conflict include:

- Policies and norms regarding relationships with suppliers
- Affirmative action guidelines
- Performance problems with drug abusers
- "Expediting" delivery and sale of products in foreign countries
- Objective versus subjective criteria for hiring
- Fairness of performance evaluations across departmental lines

The point is that this is the realm of value-based decision making. Ordinarily, decision makers within an organization agree with the stated ground rules—the official working principles. But solving specific questions or problems is often more difficult. Not only do your own principles come into play, but other stakeholder interests must be considered—the most potent being those of the organization itself. And specific dilemmas with unique and varied circumstances are rarely treated in company guidelines. As we saw in Chapter 3, many organizations clearly state their general purpose, values, and principles. But I find few issue-specific guidelines for individual managers available in official documents. Even if there were specific guidelines, each issue or dilemma is unique, so official statements could only begin to guide you toward solutions. Decision makers must have the ability to formulate value-based decisions themselves in particular situations. The "call" is often yours alone.

## Outside Challenges to Organizations

Whole organizations, as well as individuals, can feel the challenge to their working values and principles from stakeholders. R. J. Reynolds Tobacco Company, Exxon, Johnson & Johnson, A. H. Robins, and Planned Parenthood of America all found themselves facing serious issues that involved various segments of society. Each segment represented concerned stakeholders. In response to these challenges, all the companies, meeting at high executive levels, made decisions for action based on their own particular working principles.

1. R. J. Reynolds, in the face of opposition to its advertising campaigns, defended itself with the principle that the manufacture, advertising, and sale of tobacco products was legal within certain regulations.
2. Exxon's oil spill went from corporate accident to environmental tragedy. The company—far from satisfying many of its critics—pledged to aid in the cleanup of Prince William Sound.
3. Johnson & Johnson, in the famous Tylenol scare, went to the first paragraph of its guiding document, cited its responsibility to the mothers and fathers who use its products, and pulled Tylenol capsules from store shelves.
4. A. H. Robins suppressed its research findings and denied the allegations of infection resulting from use of its Dalkon Shield.
5. Planned Parenthood defended its principles concerning

the right to abortion against attack by right-to-life groups.

Organizational actions in the marketplace of stakeholders often raise serious ethical issues. And right or wrong, fitting or not, important decisions are made—have to be made—within organizations concerning these issues.

## Conflict From Norms

There can also be serious conflict around unofficial norms within an organization—the way business is *really* done. Often, norms put pressure on you as a decision maker to circumvent or disregard the stated organizational values and principles, as well as your personal principles. You can hear a common norm in action: "We don't usually do it this way, but this situation is very sensitive; we really don't have a choice." But if threatening norms are faced with candor and openness and given no power, you and your organization experience greater unity, consensus, and strength. If negative norms are not dealt with, there can be extensive divisiveness, hesitancy, hurt, and weakening of the organization.

> "Corporations have big meetings around dynamic and dangerous situations, but never even recognize small cancers inside the company—meanness, gossip, distrust, hatred—which are destroying the organization."
> —James Shannon, former executive director, General Mills Foundation

With so much at stake, and from so many sources, there are bound to be conflicts of interests from within and without. And where there are competing interests, there is a clash of values, of principles, of how business gets done around here. Many of the competing interests, other than negative norms, have validity. Many come with good arguments and clout. And most affect not only things, but people.

There are, then, not just simple, ordinary business issues.

There are clashes of balanced interests and values. There are dilemmas that must be solved.

## Dilemmas: The "Stuff" of Ethics

Consideration of organizational dilemmas takes us into the "gray zone" of business and professional life, where things are no longer black or white and where ethics has its vital role today.

A dilemma is literally an ambiguous proposition, a situation that requires a choice between equally balanced arguments, or a predicament that seemingly defies a satisfactory solution. In organizational terms, *a dilemma is a situation in which two or more options for action, representing varied interests, seem equally arguable, and where the decision is important but neither clear nor simple.*

Many organizational decisions evolve from issues, which are more abstract or general than concrete dilemmas. Issues are fairly easy to identify: accounting procedures, government regulations, affirmative action, fair hiring, customer service, targeted advertising, crisis management, sexual harassment, racial equality, community spirit, quality, and treatment of grievances, to name a few. Issues stand outside of specific circumstances and often assume that individuals or groups can do the right thing if they so intend. Issues are often about things—materials, plans, buildings, locations—rather than about specific circumstances and people.

But once you become deeply involved in particular issue situations, you begin to come across actual dilemmas. Two factors are tip-offs that you are facing both a dilemma and an ethical dilemma. First, the alternatives or options seem equally balanced—a predicament where varied stakeholders have equally strong, conflicting positions. That's a dilemma. Second, the decision for action, when it is made, will have an important impact on the welfare of people. That is the ethical factor. You could express the equation as follows: A number of valid stakeholders plus significant effects of an action on the welfare of people equals an ethical dilemma.

The ethical factor bears on "little" actions as well as "big" ones. *Any action must be viewed as having ethical implications if it affects people to any significant degree.* I don't know how often I've heard that actions have ethical implications only if they are big and sweeping, or of wide and serious import—like actions involving stock market scandal, war, medical malpractice, apartheid in South Africa, serial murder, or sexual misconduct. Granted, these have serious ethical implications, but so do *any* actions that have a substantial effect on others. This is true even if the actions seem small, such as your routine decisions in the workplace that affect people other than yourself.

Managers, when asked, usually say they can't recall an ethical dilemma they've faced! After some time spent in discussion, they realize that real dilemmas are not just about South Africa or the larger problems handled by major executives. Rather, ethical dilemmas exist in situations they themselves must decide—situations that affect the welfare and interests of people in their own surroundings. Only gradually do decision makers at every level realize that ethical dilemmas face them every day in the course of their ordinary routine. Gone is the notion that value-based decision making is concerned only with violence, theft, or a hefty dose of white-collar crime about to make headlines.

My experience indicates that most of the ethical issues presented to managers involve human resources treatment of employee problems, followed in frequency by problems involving customers and suppliers, and then conflicts between personal values and company loyalty. Most of these issues will involve ethical dilemmas.

## A Case in Point

Look at a true case that illustrates an ethical dilemma. Hank Jones owns a small air charter service. His biggest customer is a large manufacturing company that flies managers to widely separated plants. One of Hank's pilots regularly flies the CEO, and as a result of an offhand conversation, the CEO learns that the pilot is gay. The next day, the CEO calls Hank and demands that the pilot be fired. If not, Hank will lose the CEO's business.

At least on the face of it, either option presents a predicament to Hank that seems to defy a satisfactory solution. Hank has an ethical dilemma on his hands. What is satisfactory about either firing a highly competent employee or losing his biggest client? That's the business dilemma. And the alternatives seriously affect people—Hank, his employees, the pilot and his family, and Hank's suppliers. That makes it an ethical dilemma also.

Hank and you might immediately argue that the CEO doesn't have a valid claim, but it obviously seems valid enough to the CEO. There's a real clash between two different sets of stakeholder values and principles. And Hank has to decide what to do. What's important for you to see is this: Stakeholders act from differing values; differing, competing, arguable stakes are the "stuff" of ethical dilemmas.

Hank is in a real bind, as is the case with most ethical dilemmas. He would prefer not to choose either option: upholding the "larger good" of his company's future (and thus his own welfare and that of his employees and suppliers) or standing up for the individual—his pilot. The process of deciding difficult dilemmas like this is presented to you in later chapters.

The choices for action that represent competing claims are often difficult, involved, many-faceted, and filled with consequences. There is often no clear-cut or "correct" answer. You will be pulled in two directions. These are the tough ones in the gray zone. They happen every day. Occasionally, they are large in scope and consequences; more often, they are small, but important to someone. Hank's dilemma was awfully important to him, and to others.

Does any of this sound familiar? Does each and every situation you face represent a major bottom-line decision of immense proportions? No. Do some? Yes. Are they all important? Yes—to someone. Is the ability to make not only the big decisions but also the smaller, everyday ones important to your work? Of course—that's what you're there to do.

## Examples of Ethical Problem Areas

There are certain operational areas in organizations that can give rise to ethical issues and dilemmas. For instance, problems arise when an organization has a policy with no distinctions between bribery of high officials and gratuities for expedited delivery of products. How do you handle supplier relationships that involve gifts, meals, and trips? You may well face problems of fairness and equality in performance evaluation criteria, especially across departmental lines. Dealing with institutional racism and sexism can give you decision-making challenges, as can affirmative action goals viewed as reverse discrimination.

I've found three general areas that, according to decision makers, give rise to ethical dilemmas:

1. Fairness surrounding treatment of employees
2. International issues involving cultural differences
3. Role responsibility (exemplified in the statement "We make computers, period; we're not an agency of social workers")

The Conference Board, Inc., surveyed upper executives in twenty-one hundred American and foreign companies in 1987.[1] CEOs of major companies were asked which of twenty-seven highly visible issues also involved ethical considerations for business. The issues chosen by the CEOs fell into four general categories, with specific situations given. They were: (1) *equity* (basic fairness), when executive salary scales are sometimes thirty or forty times higher than that of the lowest-paid worker; (2) *rights* (treatments to which one has a just claim) with regard to due process, employee health screening, employee privacy, affirmative action, sexual harassment, shareholder interests, and whistleblowing; (3) *honesty* (integrity and truthfulness of actions or policies), which encompasses such issues as misleading advertising, financial and cash management, gifts for foreign officials, the obligation of employees to observe company and community standards, use of proprietary information for personal gain, and conflict of interest in activities outside the workplace; and (4) *exercise of corporate power*, as in support of policy positions through political action committees, adherence to standards for workplace and environmental safety, and support of the more controversial positions advocated by religious and political groups.

In summary, you face important issues and dilemmas in your work every day. The stakeholders are many and varied, and they have balanced interests that must be considered. Issues and dilemmas have ethical ramifications once they affect people in significant ways. Dilemmas, stakeholder interests, a world that is not black or white but gray, and a set of working principles—these factors make up the raw material of value-based decision making. What ethics is, and how it relates to your work, are next.

## Finding Out About Yourself

To personalize the ideas in this chapter, take a look at your own work situation by answering the following questions. The effort will give you a feel for dilemmas in your own work setting.

1. In your organization, what work areas seem to generate issues that affect the welfare of people for whom you are responsible? Examples: personnel, evaluations, personal relationships, management styles, work conditions, suppliers, customer relations, selling.

   _____

   _____

   _____

   _____

2. Name a specific situation in which your personal values and principles clashed with the organization's way of doing things.

   _____

   _____

   _____

   _____

3. Recall a dilemma in which you were the decision maker, several stakeholders had equally arguable interests, and the decision was tough to make.

_____

_____

_____

_____

4. How did you decide that dilemma? What values and
   principles did you call on for a choice of action?

_____

_____

_____

_____

## Note

1. Ronald E. Berenbeim, *Corporate Ethics*, research report from the
   Conference Board, no. 900 (1987), pp. 2–3.

# 5

# Ethics as a Creative Business Skill

## A New Organizational Definition

A defense contractor was found to be overcharging the government and was heavily penalized. Top executives put together a code of ethics spelling out employee dos and don'ts. Employees were called to half-hour meetings by division; the code was read to them, and they were told to sign a statement that they understood the code and would follow it. That is ethics—in confusion.

Some years ago, a health care products company launched a campaign to market its baby oil as a tanning product—beautifully positioning a product in two markets. But preliminary research suggested that tanning, sped up by baby oil, could possibly be harmful to the skin. When a researcher mentioned this to the vice-president of marketing, the campaign to market baby oil as a tanning product was immediately reconsidered. That is ethics—in action.

The first company did not really understand what organizational ethics is. The second did. The difference in their understanding is a matter of clearly defining ethics and its practical organizational role. That understanding is vital to your value-based decision making.

To change ethics in confusion to ethics in action, you need a clear, working, practical idea of what ethics is. There is

immense confusion in organizations about the nature of ethics
as it applies to them. For most organizations, ethics is simply a
set of mandated legal requirements and perhaps moral rules to
be followed; for all too few, it is an ongoing process of value-
based decision making. This chapter gives you a new, realistic,
working definition of organizational ethics. The definition will
cause you to rethink decision making in today's complex, morally murky organizational world. It will also prepare you for the
three-step decision-making process to come.

> "Ethics is not finding out what the correct moral
> decision is. Ethics is making, fashioning, creating
> a moral decision for action."
> —Dr. Larry Goodwin, ethicist and manager

# Fears and Misunderstandings of Ethics

A manager must understand and internalize a definition of
management before he or she can begin to manage effectively.
Similarly, to move from an ethics in confusion to an ethics in
action, you need to adopt a practical working definition of ethics.
That definition is necessary for you to make effective value-
based decisions, let alone responsible and defensible decisions.

   Most businesspeople describe ethics as "finding out" a
morally correct decision, rather than "creating" a decision for
action. In support of that contention are some descriptions of
ethics I have heard or read:

- The eternal truths of right and wrong
- Rules, really—rules of behavior
- Integrity, which starts from within
- Conformity to the standards of a professional group
- Doing what's right (or) doing what's right for you (or)
  doing what's right for you as long as you don't hurt
  someone else
- The application of what's lawful to our actions and the
  avoidance of what's unlawful

- Whatever each person wants it to be or, under pressure, needs it to be
- What the organization says it is

These current descriptions of ethics are reactive rather than proactive, and they attempt to "find" a solution instead of making one. But ethics is not like a treasure hunt in which someone, reacting to a set of clues, frantically searches for a prize hidden out there somewhere. Ethics looks ahead at a unique problem and fashions a unique moral solution. Ethics is also far more complex than simple conformity to rules or personal situational license for any behavior. Certainly, ethics concerns integrity and eternal truths, but it essentially applies them in creating a decision for action here and now in this specific situation. It demands that you make a personal choice, not find one.

This "searching for the right answer" mentality can be seen in reactions to the word itself. *Ethics,* like few other words, brings out varied reactions, all the way from "Man, could our company use more of that!" to "An ethics discussion? Give me a break! I need a negotiations workshop, not ethics." One could announce a seminar on sales techniques and fill a room in no time. Suggest a seminar on business ethics and there is a tangible wariness in the air—and plenty of empty seats!

At times, it's almost as if the word *ethics* itself were the key to a closet full of personal and corporate skeletons—as if ethics were lurking just around the corner, poised to reveal our corporate sins. These reactions are present despite a Touche Ross opinion survey of key business leaders, which found that 94 percent of respondents believe the business community as a whole is troubled by ethical problems. At the same time, the survey found that 97 percent believe American business is ethical.[1]

Yet, in spite of vague, partial definitions and ideas, a strong ethical tradition exists in organizations, industry, and society as a whole. Despite the continual accounts of individual and corporate violence to common ethical standards, there is an abiding belief in the necessity of living and working ethically. Even given the wariness of discussing ethics in the wake of lurid scandals—from Prince William Sound to the S&L debacle—

Americans and their organizations persistently desire to live, work, and be treated with integrity. As a public, we are quick to react privately and in the media to what is perceived as unethical behavior. When queried, most people and organizations say they are more ethical than others. Is there a sort of moral schizophrenia at work here? Why the wariness, even apprehension, about ethical discussion while we hold to such strong ethical traditions?

## Two Mind-Sets at Work

It seems to me there are two perceptions operating, one real and the other ideal. One is what organizational people actually know about ethics and try to use; the other is what organizational people feel about ethics and wish to use.

As to the first perception, most people in organizations are just not sure what business ethics really means in a practical, usable way. "Businesspeople just don't know what the heck ethics is, much less how it applies to their work," says one business executive. Others will admit in a moment of candor that ethics "has little if anything to do with business; you can't be too good and expect to win in this league—good guys finish last."

A number of executives argue that ethical considerations are "inappropriate" for management decisions because the "potential connection between ethical commitments and social problems can make a company a target for pressure groups." Other people just don't know how ethics fits into everyday work life: "I can't think of any ethical issues or dilemmas I've faced," says a middle manager. And most businesspeople, whether private entrepreneurs or members of organizations, have no formal training in recognizing, confronting, and solving ethical problems.

Most organizational problems are not even viewed as having ethical factors. I don't know how many times I have heard, "I just manage ordinary people in getting the job done. I don't decide what to do about selling technology to South Africa or the Middle East; *that's* ethics." It's a matter of how little is known about the nature of ethics and its application to business situations.

The second perception is what people feel about ethics in the workplace and wish they could use. It's curious that many "think ethically" as a matter of course in family life, church-related activities, public art, the entertainment media, and sexual practices. But they don't have that same "ethical sense" in work situations—until something is done to them that they perceive as harmful and "unethical." Sir Adrian Cadbury of Schweppes PLC counters that business is "part of the social system and we cannot isolate the economic elements of major decisions from their social consequences."[2]

Many businesspeople, including those in organizations, feel strongly about the ethical factors present in work and wish the meaning of ethics were clear, recognized, and applicable more than it is. Based on my experiences, here are some existing realities to consider:

- Most business and organizational people want to work with integrity.
- Most, but not all, organizations try to conduct business as ethically as possible. They attempt to make decisions that follow from moral values and principles, despite the pressures and uncertainties inherent in the marketplace today.
- Organizations and their individual members want to be treated with integrity by others—indeed, they demand it. It's interesting that both individuals and organizations, when asked, feel it is the "other guy" who is unethical, rather than themselves.
- Finally and importantly, many businesspeople and organizations just aren't very good at applying shared ethical values and principles to decision making as a matter of routine. They would like to, but they aren't sure how, nor are they very adept at it.

When you realize that ethics involves gaining ethics skills as you would other business skills, learning a process for applying ethics skills, and creating decisions for action, then the *wish* for integrity can become integrity in *fact*.

# Other Common Notions

There are several other current ideas about ethics that have an impact on you, organizations, and how you make decisions.

## *"Ethics Is Private"*

One of the widespread notions about ethics is that its place and usefulness is in one's private, family, social, and relational life. In the private setting, practical morality applies. One's own conscience is the guide, and spouses use a joint set of shared values and opinions when things are going well. In short, the true realm of ethics and morality is not business and organization life, but the social setting: personal value systems, marriage ideals, parenting, and relationships with family, friends, and neighbors.

## *"Business Is Business"*

Another current idea is that organizational life—professional, business, company, career, wage-earning life—is different from private life. If spoken, such a viewpoint might sound like this: "Sure there are individual values in the marketplace. But organizational standards and ground rules—well, that's different. The fact is that 'business is business' in a rough, competitive, pragmatic environment. The organization has its own life—its own purpose, goals, and objectives. As a member of an organization, I am part of a system with its own ethic, where company standards, government regulations, and policies and procedures are the guidelines for action. There is a joint responsibility, but business is not the place for my own values and beliefs to be exposed or imposed. I just work here. The rules have already been determined, and I contribute to the achievement of the company goals and objectives—that's professional work life, not private life and not ethics. Business is business."

## *"Just Get the Job Done"*

The "Just get the job done" notion runs along these lines: "If there are real ethical issues in business, they are the big-impact issues, the real crunches of corporate life—like making a profit, downsizing, safety, government regulations, personnel issues, and marketing strategies. These big issues are the responsibility of upper management, boards of directors, human resources, and the legal department; they're not my problem. Sure, Bhopal, South Africa, the *Exxon Valdez* oil spill, employees held hostage in foreign countries, compensation schedules, performance evaluations, and promotion policies may have some ethical implications, but I don't decide what to do about those things. Look, I design the product. I order from suppliers. I manage Katie, Tom, and Bernie out in the plant. We deliver the stuff, inspect it, paint it, sell it—the routine things that make this company go. That's got nothing to do with ethics; that's just doing a good job without too many mistakes. That's management—trying to get the folks I supervise to get the job done. The others on top handle the rest of that big stuff."

## *"If It's Legal, It's Ethical"*

Along with "Ethics is private," "Business is business," and "Just get the job done," the other current notion is that ethics in the workplace centers around law. Here's how it sounds: "The law tells us what is right and wrong. We learn what's right and wrong from our parents, our church, and sometimes from friends—or when we're punished. Laws, the legal department, the courts, judges, and juries determine what's right or wrong in the marketplace. If it's legal, it's ethical; if it's illegal, it's unethical, but we can sure try to change the law."

> "I was raised to know the difference between right and wrong. I knew it wasn't right not to tell the truth about those things. But I didn't know it was unlawful."
> —Oliver North

I experienced a good example of "What's legal is ethical" recently. From a media report, I learned that the House of Representatives Ethics Committee in Washington had established an Office of Advice and Education. Its purpose according to the media was "to counsel increasingly nervous representatives on what is and is not permissible under new ethics rules . . . including seminars to teach representatives the ins and outs of ethics." When I called to see if they did any training on handling ethics issues, I found that the new Office of Advice and Education was staffed by lawyers. They don't do ethics training; they are there to answer House members' questions arising from the Ethics Reform Act of 1989. The lawyer staff members had no training in ethics, but a fine education in the law, I am sure. "What's legal is ethical" was the message I got.

"Ethics is private," "Business is business," "Get the job done," and "What's legal is ethical" are really statements about the peripheral place ethics holds in organizational life. "Ethics is private" and "Business is business" relegate ethics back home behind the private front door. "Get the job done" passes the ethics buck from the ranks to the boardroom and upper management. "What's legal is ethical" is simply not always true—a law sets minimal standards and can be morally questioned. All actions that are unethical and all actions that are ethical cannot be publicly codified. Laws are not a surrogate for personal moral judgment and one's actions.

I am not faulting the basic purpose of business, the basic management and production duties of working people, or the necessity of law and lawyers. Rather, I am saying that the true meaning of ethics as a tool for effective, responsible, and justifiable decision making—indeed, the meaning of ethics itself—is not understood. I am also saying that the role of ethics in organizational decisions is not utilized to the extent necessary, given today's business climate.

# The Place of Ethics

Ethics is part and parcel of the activities of personal *and* business *and* organizational life. It surrounds, encompasses, and affects almost everything you do—at home and at work. It has the capability of providing invaluable guidance to your actions as an individual and a member of an organization. Ethics is an essential component of private and social life, business as business, getting the job done, and living within the law. It is a tool businesspeople must have and use along with all the other skills of organizational life, simply because ethical factors are there in your work life, whether you deny them, disregard them, or try to bump them upstairs. Ethical factors have to be dealt with—by you. We demand ethical treatment from each other, don't we?

You need to develop a concept of ethics and an ethical process that you can apply in the marketplace while being true to two things: the body of ethical knowledge itself, and the realities of your work life. A practical, understandable, workable definition of ethics for the organizational world will help.

## A New Working Definition of Ethics

I have said that the purpose of ethics is making decisions for action that flow from your own and your organization's shared values and principles. That end or purpose cannot be realized until you know what ethics is. Here is my personal working definition:

> *Ethics is the skill of making thoughtful, professional, value-based, and fitting choices of action that affect you and others.*

Here is what each of the parts of my definition means.

• *Ethics is a skill.* It is an art, like medicine, carpentry, selling, or managing. It is not a science. It is aimed at doing something—taking a concrete action—not just knowing or thinking something. Ethics is also a learned skill, so it must be practiced until it is a habit, just as the doctor or salesperson or manager must learn and practice until the art is second nature. And like any other art or skill, it is done with varying degrees of competence. The skill of ethics is not a gift from on high or the chance result of a good genetic pool. It is a skill that takes very human situations and tries to make good moral common sense of them. It creates plans of action that will solve problems and challenges in the best way possible given a set of circumstances. It forges actions; it does not find ready-made answers.

• *Ethics makes thoughtful choices of actions.* It is a rational, thought-out work of the human mind. It uses a process of reasoning, creativity, imagination, memory, and choice. It is not guessing, not a knee-jerk response, and, most of all, not a choice of expediency. Its greatest challenge as a work of the human mind is to equally consider both narrow self-interest and the stakes, needs, and wishes of others involved in work situations.

• *Ethics is a professional skill.* It deals with organizational and business work, where you have made a commitment to act from accepted duties and responsibilities. In this sense, ethics demands just as much training and coaching as any other business skill. It demands pros, not amateurs. Professionalism also demands that the decision maker be accountable for his or her decisions and the actions that follow.

• *Ethics is concerned with value-based choices of action.* Such actions flow from and are driven by accepted values and principles. Ethics fashions principled decisions; it doesn't just make rules to be followed blindly. It takes issues and dilemmas—balanced, arguable circumstances not admitting of easy, "please 'em all" answers—and makes solutions based on values and principles. Decisions that are value-based reflect consistency, effectiveness, and responsibility, and therefore they are justifiable.

If ethics were defined as an eternal set of action-specific truths leading always to perfect right or wrong, then it would not be applicable to many real dilemmas in today's organizational world. Your world of work is not that simple. You need a skill that will help you do the best you can, given this situation, these facts, these stakeholders, these clashing values. It is a matter not of always acting perfectly—all right, no wrong, no hurt—but of creating a way that is responsible to the highest values you hold that apply now, to this murky situation.

• *Ethics is concerned with "fitting" choices for action.* In organizations and business—in the gray zone—there is not only right versus wrong, truth versus falsehood, or good against evil. Decisions that are clearly right or wrong are fairly simple. Ethics often has to deal with tough, complicated dilemmas and choices of action that reflect the most fitting answers possible here and now. An action that seems right today may be wrong tomorrow given other circumstances; or it may have other unwanted but unavoidable effects despite your best efforts. Ethics involves making the best—the most fitting—choice of action possible under unique, often very difficult, and ambiguous circumstances.

• *Ethics is concerned with decisions that affect you and others.* Contrary to the common notion that it is only about the "big issues" and not the daily routine of your life, ethics involves every action that significantly affects the welfare of people—you, me, and others. If you have an issue that in no way has a significant impact on people, then ethics is not involved. Can you name many? It may be a surprise, but almost all you do has some ethical implications. That doesn't mean every business decision you face is difficult—fraught with horrendous ethical implicatons and possibly dire results. Most are simple. But once you have a sensitivity to ethics, dilemmas take on a new look and urgency. They are far more common than you think.

# From Abstraction to Action

So now you have a new definition of ethics for business and organizations. Why should it hold any lasting importance for you? First, the definition brings ethics out of the abstract world of academia and religion; it makes ethics understandable and workable where it belongs—in the real world of your personal and professional life. Ethics has not been understood because it has often been discussed in abstract and scholarly terms, far from the ordinary jargon (and therefore practical realm) of business life.

Second, this definition makes ethics an essential part of the process of decision making. It makes ethics far more practical and applicable to ordinary, day-to-day business routine. It takes away the excuse that ethics is only what the higher-ups and the legal department handle. You handle ethical matters, too—every day! It doesn't let you say that ethics is about "those big issues at headquarters or in Washington or in some world hot spot, and that's not what I do!" You and I handle many issues and dilemmas that affect the welfare of people around us—in fact, we are part of those issues and dilemmas.

Third, this definition leads you to a process of decision making (see Chapter 8) that helps you do your work better, more successfully, and more responsibly. If you use this definition, your decision-making process can include the ethical dimension as well as the business dimension. And the process will give you justifiable or defensible decisions, for the simple reason that they will be based on commonly held General Principles as you understand them.

Ethics is not a clerical genie in a bottle, a sage on Mount Olympus, or a personal guru with all the answers. It's a tool you and I can use to be better at our work, better with our people, and better for our organizations. In the 1990s and beyond, the public will not be gentle with individuals and organizations that do not strive for integrity and show it in their actions.

Begin, then, to look at elements of the process of value-based decision making in the following chapters. You are about to put ethics into action. You are no longer dealing with an ethics in confusion.

## Finding Out About Yourself

To help you get a personal feel for my definition of ethics, try the following questions:

1. Before reading this chapter, how would you have defined personal ethics?

_____

_____

_____

_____

2. How would you have defined business ethics?

_____

_____

_____

_____

3. After reading this chapter, have your own definitions of personal and business ethics changed in any way? What would they sound like now?
My own practical definition of personal ethics is:

_____

_____

_____

_____

My own practical definition of business or organizational ethics is:

_____

_____

_____

_____

# Notes

1. *Ethics in American Business: An Opinion Survey of Key Business Leaders on Ethical Standards and Behaviors,* Touche Ross, 1988, pp. 1–2.
2. Sir Adrian Cadbury, "Ethical Managers Make Their Own Rules," *Harvard Business Review* (September/October 1987), p. 70. Copyright © 1987 by the President and Fellows of Harvard College; all rights reserved.

# 6

# The Magnificent Seven

## Checking In With the Universal General Principles

Have you noticed that people in organizations are often genuinely perplexed, even piqued, when told that most of what they do involves ethics? Maybe you are, too. True, your proper work is business decision making. But most decisions involve people, and where people are involved, as you have seen, so is ethics.

Decisions that significantly affect the welfare of people must flow from moral as well as purely business principles. As a decision maker, you constantly handle situations in which business and moral factors are inseparable. Hiring and firing, for example, are obviously financial and production issues, but they are also moral issues because they affect the lives of people directly.

Business and organizational working principles are usually included in mission statements, goals and objectives, and policy manuals. *But if decision makers must also consider ethical factors, where are common, generally accepted moral principles found?* Beyond stated company principles, are there any public, generally accepted moral guidelines to help you resolve business dilemmas that are also moral dilemmas?

This chapter answers those questions by defining and exploring some Universal General Moral Principles (the Magnificent Seven), which are a central part of value-based decision making. You will see what they are and how they are reflected in your options for action. Those options will then merge both business and moral realities. In later chapters, you will see how the Magnificent Seven guide your choice of options and fit into a new total decision-making process.

## A Case Example

Let's begin with an actual case example, which will enable you to see the Magnificent Seven in operation.

Bill's direct report secretary, Susan, is a young, single parent with two children. This is her first job outside the home, and she is not getting the required child support from the father. She is doing excellent work—in fact, she has recently been named employee of the month. Bill is relieved to finally have such a competent assistant.

One of Susan's minor responsibilities is to keep an account comprised of a fair amount of petty cash. The money is collected from use of nonmetered postage stamps and from honor donations to an informal coffee, snack, and box-lunch program. An unannounced audit is unable to account for $200 from this account.

Susan at first denies knowledge of how the money could be missing, but after Bill confronts her, she admits having "borrowed" the $200 for pressing family needs. She promises to pay the money back from her biweekly checks over several pay periods. However, the company policy and procedure manual states that theft warrants termination and possible prosecution.

Bill has a dilemma. On the one hand, his responsibility is to maintain company accounting procedures and enforce honest behavior, as mandated by company policy. On the other, his secretary has proven competencies that enhance his performance. But financial pressures and theft have compromised her work and his. Bill's decision will also form perceptions about his management in the minds of his supervisors and other employees. He may need to defend his decision to other stakeholders.

Bill could use some help beyond the policy manual, which doesn't take into account the particular circumstances of his situation. Where does he turn for guidelines?

Let's define what the Magnificent Seven are, discuss what insights they bring to decision making, and then apply them to Bill's situation.

## The Magnificent Seven and Where We Got Them

The General Moral Principles are moral common denominators. They represent the most universal statements of moral behavior that human beings have devised and accepted. They have come down through the centuries; they have been propagated, advanced, and taught by the world's major religions, dogmas, master teachers, and philosophers. The Magnificent Seven, in their general form, state what most human beings value, in some way, about life, behavior, and coexistence.

The novelist Tom Clancy once described them as "not ethereal ideas. They are, in fact, the distillation of ten thousand years of human social evolution. We have settled on them not because they are pretty but because they are the only things that work. Principle is what gives life meaning."

The Magnificent Seven are valuable as moral guidelines in decision making because they are universal, consistent, objective, and defensible. They are universal because most people would agree that they are right and acceptable and that they work. They are consistent because they have stood the test of time and are more than "here today, gone tomorrow" fad opinions. They are objective—general enough to be applicable to more than one subjective situation. Importantly, they are defensible; they are appropriate justification for action in the moral view of most people.

The Magnificent Seven are a bedrock, an unshifting touchstone of moral principles that lends clarity and solidity to your decisions for action. They make your organizational choices value-based in a moral sense, not just business-based. When you use them as touchstones and guidelines, your decisions will be *principled*. Decisions on principle are the mark of ethical choices and have an odds-on chance of being viewed as fitting, responsible, and defensible.

The Magnificent Seven are valuable because, in their most general meaning, they are universal and accepted by most people. But once they are taken beyond their most general meaning, each of us understands and interprets them differently when we apply them to particular situations. What Bill sees as fair and just may not be what the company or Susan interpets fairness and justice to mean in this particular situation. Each of us—and each organization—gives unique meanings and interpretations to how a General Principle applies to our view of the world, our value system, and our own issues and dilemmas. That is why one company may see its competitor's truthful promotion of a product as a less than honest representation of the facts.

Nevertheless, it is precisely the wide acceptance of the Universal Principles that makes them useful in ethical decision making. What makes moral decisions difficult is the need to concretely interpret the General Principles in particular situations—with interpretations that can be disputed. Let's now define and describe the Magnificent Seven.

## The Magnificent Seven

1. *Dignity of human life: The lives of people are to be respected.* Human beings, by the fact of their existence, have value and dignity. We may not act in ways that directly intend to harm or kill an innocent person. Human beings have a right to live; we have an obligation to respect that right to life. Human life is to be preserved and treated as sacred.

Immediately, more specific ideas, questions, and problems about the dignity of human life arise as we apply it to our own value systems and particular work situations. What do *life, respect,* and *harm* mean? When is someone not an "innocent" person? Are there situations when you have to harm others? Are there circumstances in your job that might cause harm to you or others? How can an organization control everything so that no harm is done to anyone? Some businesses are just dangerous; how far does safety have to go—isn't OSHA enough? Should pregnant women be allowed to hold production jobs that may endanger fetuses? Answers to these questions—interpretation and application of the dignity of human life to particular situations—differ among various people.

2. *Autonomy: All persons are intrinsically valuable and have the right to self-determination.* We should act in ways that

demonstrate each person's worth, dignity, and right to free choice. We have a right to act in ways that assert our own worth and legitimate needs. We should not use others as mere "things," or only as means to an end. Each person has an equal right to basic human liberty, compatible with a similar liberty for others.

As we think about autonomy in general, our own meanings and interpretations come into play. What happens when your autonomy impinges on someone else's self-determination? What happens when your exercise of liberty takes away from someone else's liberty? What do *value, dignity,* and *self-determination* mean to you? Morally speaking, may someone give up his or her dignity and right of self-determination?

If your business or organization makes decisions that clash with your free choice, what can you do? Do organizations have a right to act like individuals in exercising their self-determination? Do people in organizations have a right to free choices concerning their own privacy? Can companies mandate testing for the HIV virus and still honor a person's privacy?

3. *Honesty: The truth should be told to those who have a right to know it.* Honesty is also known as integrity, truth telling, and honor. One should speak and act so as to reflect the reality of the situation. Speaking and acting should mirror the way things really are. There are times when others have the right to hear the truth from us; there are times when they do not.

As you apply honesty to your own situations, you find that the resulting interpretation is not as clear as the General Principle itself. Is lying always wrong? What if a burglar demands to know where the jewels are? Can a secretary say you are in a meeting when you aren't? Who has a right to know the truth from you? When your organization asks questions that may hurt your chances of keeping your job or getting a promotion, do you have to answer honestly? In a job interview, do you have to answer all the questions honestly?

Does the IRS have a right to the truth about your income? If "a little white lie" or "bending the truth a little" will get you a whopping sale, may you do it? What if a company's truthfulness will hurt its employees and shareholders? Can you "hedge" the truth about your product if it means a huge contract and the lack of truth won't hurt the customer? Would you put the terms of your latest deal in the newspaper exactly as they were spelled out? Must you tell the truth to someone who doesn't want to know it, or can't handle it? Can an organization, an industry, a community, or a country function at all unless people generally tell the truth?

4. *Loyalty: Promises, contracts, and commitments should be honored.* Loyalty includes fidelity, promise keeping, keeping the public trust, good citizenship, excellence in quality of work, reliability, commitment, and honoring just laws, rules, and policies. One should honor and keep confidences and secrets, and protect proprietary and personal private information that is freely and willingly shared. One should fulfill written and verbal contracts and commitments. People should demonstrate trust and loyalty to friends, family, organizations, and their country. People in organizations should not steal or destroy property; they should safeguard their free judgment in business by avoiding conflicts of interest. They should fulfill just rules, laws, and policies.

As you apply loyalty to your own life and work situations, valid questions arise. What is a "just" rule, law, or company policy? When is a contract or commitment no longer binding? Can you ever break a confidence or tell a secret? Are whistle-blowers ever acting loyally toward an organization? What if loyalty endangers your job or promotion? What information can you take to a new employer from your old organization? What if you go to work for a company and never know (much less agree to) the policies and rules—how can you be loyal? What if you have to choose between loyalty to a customer or other stakeholder and loyalty to your employer?

What does "excellence in quality of work" mean? What if you don't have a written contract with your company—how do you know where your loyalty begins and ends? What about the pressures you are under to "get the job done," versus your own values and principles? To whom are you supposed to be loyal? What's a "conflict of interest," anyway? What if a bribe here at home is considered a tip in another country?

5. *Fairness: People should be treated justly.* One has the right to be treated fairly, impartially, and equitably. One has the

obligation to treat others fairly and justly. All have the right to
the necessities of life—especially those in deep need and the
helpless. Justice includes equal, impartial, unbiased treatment.
Fairness tolerates diversity and accepts differences in people
and their ideas. All employees have the right to fair treatment
under work contracts, company policies and procedures, and
the law.

As you personally define and apply fairness, many differences, questions, and problems come up. What do you mean by
*justice*? Do people ever give up the right to be treated fairly?
What do *deep need* and *helpless* mean? When can you use
another's mistakes for your own or your company's advantage?
Do some people and organizations get more fairness than others? Who comes first, the organization or the individual? How
much safety on the job is fair? Are executives sometimes treated
less fairly than those in lower positions? How does "work
privacy" relate to the right to fair treatment? Are the affirmative action policies in your organization fair? Would you be
treated fairly if you had a grievance against the organization
you work for?

Who said the world was fair, anyway? What does "necessities of life" mean? The classifieds are full of jobs—how can
someone really lack the necessities of life? Doesn't receiving
justice have something to do with how much power you have? Is
it fair that computers make decisions that have serious impact
on people, with little or no input from human beings?

6. *Humaneness:* There are two parts: (1) *Our actions ought
to accomplish good,* and (2) *we should avoid doing evil.* We
should do good to others and to ourselves. We should have
concern for the well-being of others; usually, we show this
concern in the form of compassion, giving, kindness, serving,
and caring. "Do unto others as you would have them do unto
you." We should act and speak in ways that benefit our own
valid self-interests and those of others. We must avoid actions
that are evil.

Humaneness also has many interpretations and meanings.
What is *good* and what is *evil*? Is this the real world we're
talking about? When does justice leave off and charity or caring
begin—and do they have different obligations? How do you

balance doing good for others with doing good for yourself? How can one avoid ever doing harm to others? What if doing good is not possible except by harming yourself or others? What if you have to choose between two good actions? What if you have to choose between two evil actions?

How far must you go to "care" for others? Do you have to risk your own welfare to help others? Do you have to do good to your enemies? How can the pressure of business competition today square with humaneness? Don't you always see your own self-interest as valid? How can you always care for employees and also take care of yourself? How can you always treat all your organization's stakeholders with humaneness?

7. *The common good: Actions should accomplish the "greatest good for the greatest number" of people.* One should act and speak in ways that benefit the welfare of the largest number of people, while trying to protect the rights of individuals.

Here are some questions of meaning and interpretation you will face: What about situations in which benefiting the largest number of people requires you to violate someone else's rights? What is more important, the common good of many people or someone's individual good? Which comes first—the good of the organization or the welfare of individuals within it (for example, layoffs versus risking the survival of the company itself)? How can you ever make decisions that benefit all your stakeholders, and do you have to?

How can you serve the common good when one group has preference by law? What does "the greatest good for the greatest number" mean, anyway? "He who tries to please all pleases none," right? Isn't it right that organizations must always choose their own survival and well-being over the good of others? How can you square the common good with the other six principles?

## Some Important Qualifications

The generality of the Magnificent Seven, coupled with their need for interpretation in specific situations, demands reemphasis and some additional points.

1. The utility and strength of the General Principles lie in the fact that they are abstract enough to be right for most people, wide enough to be applicable to most situations, and sufficiently powerful to justify actions. Bill will find them useful in resolving his own particular dilemma.

2. The Magnificent Seven need specific meanings and interpretation when reflected in a particular situation. Bill has to decide what he means by fairness, humaneness, and the common good. He also has to realize that Susan and the company may interpret those General Principles differently, given their own "stakes" in the situation. Bill's notion of fairness and the common good may not be fair and good in the minds of Susan and her family, and the company may interpret these principles in yet a third way.

3. Dilemmas often do not admit of clear-cut decisions that are simply right or wrong. Rather, the solution is the best choice among several options that are fitting but not perfect. Or a solution may be chosen that is not perfectly fitting but allows the accomplishment of a greater or equal benefit. In our case, one option is to fire Susan; a lesser disciplinary action might keep her valuable skills intact for the future while not condoning her dishonesty.

The General Principles force us to look seriously at the competing interests of all stakeholders. Bill does not have all the principles on his side; nor does Susan or the company. Competing interests have a better chance of consideration when viewed through the prism of the Magnificent Seven—in this case honesty, fairness, humaneness, and the common good.

4. Circumstances—specific facts, motives, pressures, demands, and needs that relate to a situation—are relevant to complex decisions. While the General Principles provide a context of solid values translatable to the situation, the specific facts demand interpretation and application of those relevant principles. Bill will ask what particular principle or principles are most important here in this situation. Is it fairness or humaneness or others? Is it a combination of several?

5. The Magnificent Seven are powerful guidelines because one or more of them will be seen as a morally defensible reason for chosen actions. The choice of which principles to apply in

any given situation rests with you, the decision maker. Bill will choose an option that, because it represents one or more General Principles most important to him, is morally defensible.

## Application to Bill's Dilemma

Bill has several options. One is to terminate Susan, using company principles and policies backed up by the General Principles of strict fairness and honesty. This would set an example for other employees and exercise autonomy—both his and the company's.

Humaneness as well as fairness could be interpreted in support of another option. As Bill looks at the particular circumstances of Susan's theft, he could weigh the financial pressures she is under against the harm done to the company and his department. Could these circumstances lessen the demand for strict fairness and termination? How would Bill's supervisors and other employees view an option less than termination?

Bill's own self-interest and autonomy might call for an option less than termination—Susan has fine skills and has performed well for him. Could an option of reprimand and probation honor justice but still humanely preserve her valued services and her need for a job?

All of Bill's options are arguable and defensible, considered in the light of *his* business principles and the meaning and importance of the Magnificent Seven as *he* sees them. In a real dilemma, there is no one absolute answer separate from the decision maker. Application of the Magnificent Seven ensures that Bill's own decision is fitting, principled, and defensible for him—even if it's not perfect, and even if it's different from what yours and mine would be. There is no definitive answer outside of each person's process of creating his or her own decision. That personal process is what's important here, not the argument over respective solutions.

The more you and others in organizations internalize the Magnificent Seven—defining their meanings as part of your ground rules—the better your solutions to dilemmas will be. Dilemmas are rarely resolved easily or perfectly. The Magnificent Seven not only make those resolutions possible, they make them justifiable and the best outcomes you can attain.

If you have difficulty prioritizing the General Principles, the discussion of ethical systems in Chapter 7 will help.

## Finding Out About Yourself

Using the Magnificent Seven is probably not a conscious part of what you ordinarily do in handling business/ethical dilemmas. It should be. In light of this chapter, try your hand at the following:

**Dilemma:** A strong prospect for computer sales manager comes before the executive selection committee for a final interview. You are chairperson of the committee. The candidate gives you a complete list of his current employer's clients, including their present system needs, their projected future needs, and recommended pricing.

1. Who are the stakeholders in this situation?

   _____

   _____

   _____

   _____

2. Which of the Magnificent Seven apply to this dilemma?

   _____

   _____

   _____

   _____

3. Which principle or principles have the highest priority in your solution as you see it?

   _____

   _____

_____

_____

   **Dilemma:** A company that produces defense munitions needs
to test them. An uninhabited area that can be leased from the
government is chosen as the test site. When plans for the tests are
made public, a Native American tribe objects, claiming the land
is an ancient and sacrd burial ground. You must solve the problem.

1. Who are the stakeholders in this situation?

   _____

   _____

   _____

   _____

2. Which of the Magnificent Seven apply to this dilemma?

   _____

   _____

   _____

   _____

3. Which principle or principles has or have the highest priority
   in your solution as you see it?

   _____

   _____

   _____

   _____

# 7

# Moral Attitudes for Decision Making

## Ranking General Principles and Options

Seeing the connection between an option for action and one or more of the Magnificent Seven is a key step in value-based decision making. General Principles—represented in your options for action—give morality to your actions.

But immediately you face a problem that is peculiar to the business skill of ethics. When you join General Principles to options for action, the General Principles admit of differing interpretations, and they can conflict with one another in specific situations. How, then, as you consider all the stakeholders seriously, do you prioritize General Principles and options as to importance in your situation? Let's begin to address the problem with an example.

You need to cut your work force in the face of declining sales. You know the facts of the situation, and you see the General Principles reflected in your options: Autonomy and the common good of the company support the option to cut personnel; fairness and humaneness support the stakeholder interests of employees threatened with losing their jobs. Thus, these principles conflict with one another: for example, autonomy versus fairness. But which of them are most important in your situation? How do you rank them in importance, so that the option represented is the most fitting choice for you to make?

# The Need for a System

You need a system—a moral perspective or attitude—that helps you prioritize the General Principles and their options. Such a perspective would allow you to choose the most principled option. Traditionally, there have been two moral systems for ranking action options. One concerns the correctness of actions themselves; the other looks to the results or consequences of actions. I call them the Action Itself System and the Results System.

# The Two Systems: An Example

You are the sole heir of a close friend's estate, which includes a company she owns completely. The two of you are hiking one day, and your friend has a massive heart attack. With her last few breaths, she asks you to see to it that the company is given to a beloved companion. Now you know this man is a drug addict and a gambler; he is totally incapable of handling himself, much less a company. You know that he will squander or ruin the company. You can foresee the dire consequences if you honor the promise. But if you break the promise and do something better with the company, the results will be good, and your friend will never know. What should you do?

Honoring the friend's promise, no matter what the result, is an example of the Action Itself System. The second alternative, looking to the results of your promise if followed, is an example of the Results System.

## *The Action Itself System*

This moral attitude for decision making holds that an action is correct or incorrect because of the *very nature of the action itself*. An action is fitting or unfitting in itself—not because of the results, circumstances, or intentions of the action. Lying, stealing, and killing are wrong because there is something intrinsically wrong with those acts. Period. Therefore, telling the truth, not stealing, and not killing are simply right, correct, and fitting.

In the case example, you would fulfill the request of your dying friend simply because you promised to do so. It would be wrong not to. This system would say that any business decision and action that violates the General Moral Principles directly is incorrect, unfitting, or wrong.

---

### The Action Itself System

*Emphasis:* individual rights and duties.
*Its motto:* "Only actions right in themselves should be done."

---

This system doesn't initially look to the common good of the many for the correctness of an action. It says that one can never violate an individual's right—even to promote the common good of all, or a greater good.

The Action Itself System can often be the right answer to a situation. Examples of such situations include an organization's adherence to a just law that ensures basic worker safety, or employee adherence to a prohibition against theft. The Action Itself System's main drawback is that it can sometimes be too rigid. The system is difficult to use in a true dilemma because it can violate other strong General Principles. If you strictly followed the Action Itself System, you could not lie to a burglar to save your property; you couldn't kill someone who attacked your family. You could not have your secretary tell a caller that you are in a meeting when, indeed, you are not; that would be lying. You would be bound to total honesty even if it damaged you or others. You would give your dying friend's company to her companion because you promised you would, and a promise must be kept.

*The Opposite Scenario*

If those examples strain your common sense or survival instincts, think what problems would result if important players in your business world rarely told the truth or honored the rights of individuals. There would be utter chaos. Nothing would be accomplished. The very structure, activity, and progress of business and social life rest on mutual trust—trust that people will, in fact, live and work within the mandates of the General Principles, at least in their most general form.

### *The System's Limitations*

Consider how Johnson & Johnson managed the Tylenol capsules scare some years ago. The company's management was not operating solely out of the Action Itself System of decision making. If it had been, it could have concluded that making, packaging, and distributing Tylenol capsules continued to be ethically legitimate, despite the tampering. Someone else outside of the company's control was criminally poisoning the capsules, and that individual should be dealt with by the retail stores and law enforcement.

The Action Itself System works well enough when there are no complicating circumstances or foreseeable harmful consequences. But given competing stakeholders and unintended results, the Action Itself System can be rigid and limiting. A decision to move a plant to another city, based simply on the action in itself and a company's autonomy, seems fitting enough. But other stakeholders—the community, suppliers, local merchants, employees, families—see the results of the decision subverting General Principles important to them. Their autonomy, fairness, and the common good are equally valuable to them. Both options have stakeholder validity; both are reflected in General Principles. The company option looks mainly at the correctness of its action in itself and not at the consequences for others.

In summary, the Action Itself System, while looking to the General Principles, asks whether an action is correct, fitting, or right in and of itself, without first taking into account the circumstances or consequences of such a decision. It is demanding, because its motivation is to choose what is simply right, or not choose what is simply wrong. This system alone, in a dilemma situation, can be rigid and restrictive in a world teeming with complexities, important circumstances, and weighty consequences.

"There are times, demanding courage, when one chooses
to do what is simply right. Not because there is no other
choice, but simply because it is right. Only afterwards does
one realize there really was no other way."
                                                    —Author unknown

## The Results System

The Results System holds that an action is correct or incorrect
primarily because of the *consequences* or results of the action.
What the action causes to happen is paramount. The key ele-
ment is not the nature of the action itself, but its effect. In case
of your dying friend's last request, you would have to consider
what would probably happen if the companion got control of
your friend's company. The consequences would be disastrous,
and there should be the option of doing something other than
what was promised.

When you use this system, it is important to project the
decision into the future and try to foresee what effects the action
will have. Those effects determine the correctness, the fitting-
ness, the rightness of the decision and its action.

The Results System looks first to the aim, the goal, the end
of an action decision. While the Action Itself System looks at
individual rights and obligations, the Results System emphasizes
the effects of an action on outcomes and multiple stakeholders.
It tends to favor "the greatest good for the greatest number."

Under this system, you would not have to tell a burglar the
truth about where your jewelry is. You could do whatever was
necessary to stop a brutal attack on your family. Under certain
circumstances, your secretary could say you are in a meeting
when you are not. Why are these answers different from the
ones give earlier? Because this system, unlike the first, emphasizes the results of an action as the key determinant of that
action's fitness. You would probably find a new owner for your
dying friend's company rather than fulfill your spur-of-the-mo-
ment promise.

---

### The Results System

*Emphasis:* the common good of many.
*Its motto:* "One is accountable for the
consequences of actions."

---

Johnson & Johnson applied the Results System, in the form of its credo of responsibilities, to the Tylenol problem and quickly came to a conclusion. The effect of the company's product, poisoned by someone, was to endanger the lives of its customers. Johnson & Johnson chose to remove all distributed capsules and later replaced them with safer caplets.

McDonald's Corporation recently decided to change its burger containers from polystyrene "clamshells" to cardboard. It replaced the old packaging, which in the eyes of many consumers was environmentally unacceptable. The wishes of stakeholders—in this case, customers—were heard over the advantages of an Action Itself decision. Customer perceptions are sometimes also a consequence!

If the companies associated with thalidomide, the Dalkon Shield, and asbestos had tested their products more thoroughly, paid more attention to the existing research, and looked earlier at the possible consequences of their decisions, how different their marketing histories might have been!

In summary, the Results System, while looking to the General Principles, impels the decision maker to ask whether the action decision is correct or fitting based on a projection of its consequences. It is demanding in the sense that one has to be proactive and imaginative, picturing possible consequences and their effects on self and others. Its danger: In considering only the results of a particular action—which may be good—one can miss the fact that the action itself may be wrong for other reasons. This pitfall shows up in the following examples:

• Removing highly toxic wastes from close proximity to plant workers (an action with the good consequence of worker safety) by dumping them onto the open ground some distance away (not a good action due to pollution)

- Cutting a financially troubled airline's operating expenses by delaying required maintenance repairs
- Driving a competitor out of business by lying or illegal means

## Both Systems Used in Tandem

Except in situations where an action itself is clearly right or wrong, or where no serious consequences or varied stakeholder interests are involved, it is increasingly rare to find an organization adhering tenaciously to one or the other of these systems. In practice, the two systems are usually found in combination. The reason for this involves simple practicality as well as ethical theory. Both systems are necessary today for effective decision making in a complex, ever-changing international marketplace inhabited by myriad stakeholders, laws, customs, circumstances, and dangers as well as opportunities. No longer can individuals and organizations apply only one of these systems and necessarily expect to get an acceptable and defensible solution. In today's business climate, serious errors can be made by following one of these systems exclusively.

### Gaining the "Moral High Ground"

Today, you may feel the pressure of interest groups who use one of the two systems in order to gain the moral high ground. Someone has called this phenomenon the "ethical superiority of the uninvolved." The term *uninvolved* means that single-interest groups don't have to consider all the circumstances you face in a given situation, even though their interest as stakeholders may have validity. You can sometimes co-opt the moral high ground by using the two systems in tandem. By doing this, you can not only make a responsible and fitting decision for action, but also defend the decision on ethical grounds.

## The Responsibility System

I would like to present a new approach to value-based decision making, called the Responsibility System. This system doesn't replace the two better-known systems. Instead, it incorporates them into a new moral attitude that is more responsive to today's marketplace diversity and complexity.

> "We are still incapable of understanding that the only genuine backbone of our actions, if they are to be moral, is responsibility."
> —Vaclav Havel, President of Czechoslovakia, to the U.S. Congress, February 21, 1990

I define the Responsibility System as *a moral attitude for decision making that ranks the General Principles and options for action based on mutual cooperation with others.*

With this system, an action is fitting or unfitting, correct or incorrect, based on whether—in a spirit of cooperation and goodwill—it responds to the legitimate mutual needs you and others have. The system is born of the realization that we need each other in order to survive, succeed, and be better than we are. If you are to survive and prosper, you must be "response-able" to my wish to survive and prosper.

This attitude for decision making is part of the skill of ethics that creates cooperative answers to complex human and business problems. It means coming to terms with needs and desires we have in common and emphasizing those, rather than our differences. It is a system practiced among people who have individual rights and freedoms, but who must be interdependent as well as independent if they want to be better than they are.

> ## The Responsibility System
> *Emphasis:* mutual cooperation.
> *Its motto:* "I can succeed better with you, and you with me."

### The Social Roots of Responsibility

The idea of responsibility is not new, but deliberately using it to make moral organizational decisions is. The word *responsibility* literally means "a promise to answer in return." It denotes the ability to make rational business decisions that respond to the welfare of others as well as to our own. It connotes an adult responsibility *to* other people, but not *for* them.

Responsibility exists right where you work. Think about the duties of your job, your challenges, the things you have to decide—your "responsibilities." These aspects of your position demand ethical decision making. The patterns of responsibility are built into the activities and relationships you have now. What we and organizations have to do is make responsibility a conscious, overall attitude for decision making.

A good example of responsibility as a management attitude is the story of General Motors' new car company, Saturn. The way Saturn manages people from the perspective of responsibility represents a profound change in style and use of cooperation. The executive suite is shared by Saturn's president and the United Auto Workers coordinator. They travel and conduct the company's business together. But beyond their sharing of top power, a labor agreement has established over one hundred work teams, which are given wide responsibility. They interview and approve new hires for their teams. They decide how to run their own areas, shut down the entire assembly line when a problem arises, and have budget responsibility. The Saturn philosophy is a team commitment to decisions before changes are put in place, from choosing an ad agency to selecting outside suppliers. While not precisely and consciously the Responsibility System that I'm outlining here, the radical change in the way GM manages people is a concept of "shared responsibility" put into practice through decision making.

> "I stressed all along that organization does not deal with power, but with responsibility."
>
> —Peter Drucker

Here is a powerful idea you ought to seriously consider as a working person, a member of an organization, and a decision maker: Responsibility—as an overall attitude for decision making—can meld values, principles, and effort into a more unified, successful, and justifiable way of doing business. How? By making *cooperation*—the heart of responsibility—work in your choices for action.

## The Meaning of Cooperation

Cooperation is possible because it's demanded by who we are as human beings. It is our basic nature to be selfish—to be primarily self-interested. But to take care of ourselves also demands that we be unselfish—interested in the welfare of others.

### Selfishness Is OK

Selfishness is the most ancient characteristic of life. The driving force of each cell in our bodies is its own survival and growth. Our first instinct is to preserve and foster our own well-being. All our choices and actions are primarily aimed at our own self-interest. That's not wrong; it's just the way it is. Acknowledging our basic self-interest is important, because self-interest explains the formation of our values and principles and the way we make decisions in life and work. It explains why, in organizational life, others always seem to take care of number one, and why others see us as taking care of number one. The conclusion is clear: You and I are going to take care of ourselves; organizations are going to take care of themselves. That's primary. That's the way life is. It's also not enough.

### Selflessness Is OK

Curiously, despite our inborn selfishness, most of us are also unselfish as well. Early in life, we learn that to survive, grow, and prosper, we need more than ourselves. We cannot really "go it alone." We learn that the help of others is absolutely necessary if we are to make it in life. At some point, it dawns on me that if I am to survive and be better than I am, I need you. And you need me if you are to survive and be better than you are. We realize that independence has to include interdependence.

*Putting Selfishness and Selflessness Together*

Since we cannot "go it alone," we begin to interact with others, just as the cells of our bodies interact with other cells, organs, and systems for our total benefit. We relate to other people—supplying what they need to survive, grow, and prosper—so that we, in return, may gain what we need.

With that mutuality of self-interest, we can both be better than we are alone. Our interest and investment in others generates their goodwill, so that they will help us again. Their help creates goodwill in us, which motivates us to help them again. Independence and interdependence, selfishness blended with selflessness, is cooperation.

But isn't the expectation of mutual cooperation unrealistic, if not naive? I think not, if the motive for cooperation is ultimately self-interest. There is nothing in life and work more realistic than that. An unacceptable mistake is failure to mutually become the best we can be. Certainly we and organizations will not be able to cooperate with everyone else. But lack of cooperation should be the exception, not the rule. Don't call naive what has rarely been tried.

## Moral Responsibility as Cooperation

My argument for a more workable system for ethical, principled decision making is this: Responsibility is more than just a good management philosophy. It speaks to both the variety of existing moral beliefs and the complexity of the marketplace today. As a moral attitude for decision making, responsibility is possible and practical because it utilizes what is most basic in our nature: our self-interest. As a moral system, it also demands mutual cooperation, to my benefit *and* yours; selfishness alone won't work anymore, if it ever did. Responsibility is the way each of us "answers" and "promises a response" to another.

Responsibility gives us permission to act from basic natural drives—selfishness coupled with selflessness. I think a truly workable system for moral decision making today operates from motives most natural and common to all human beings. And what of the higher motives we may have as human beings? Any civic, spiritual, and religious values that encourage cooperative responsibility only add to its success as a moral attitude for decision making.

Responsibility does not mean license to "cooperate" in the sense of collusion, unfair competition, oppression, "anything goes" strategies, and the rest of the list. Why shouldn't those things happen with this system? Because true responsibility is a moral attitude, joining options for action and General Moral Principles, as you saw earlier in this chapter. If the possible options are totally unprincipled morally, they won't connect to the General Principles of dignity of human life, fairness, honesty, autonomy, loyalty, humaneness, and the common good—and you'll know it. Such an effort will just be a useless exercise, with no feeling of personal integrity or honesty with yourself.

## Applying the Responsibility System

How, then, does the Responsibility System help you rank the Magnificent Seven General Principles as part of a decision-making process? First, it adopts the overall moral attitude of responsible cooperation, for your benefit and mine, as a business way of thinking. Then, in the face of a dilemma, it asks: *What General Principle or Principles, reflected in each option for action, are the most responsible in my situation?* Asked in Step 3 of the process to come (see Chapter 8), that question—if it embodies the meaning of cooperation as a moral business attitude—would include both the correctness of the action itself and the correctness of the consequences. The answer would point you to the most principled option for action.

Responsibility—not necessarily as the moral system defined here, but as a shared business value—is why Johnson & Johnson's executives were quickly able to choose an option in response to the Tylenol problem. J&J's *Our Credo* is stated and followed in terms of the company's responsibilities. The answer to the question in the preceding paragraph allows you to resolve the dilemma of your dying friend's request. It's why adherence to just laws can be seen as responsible. As a moral business attitude, it gives McDonald's Corporation a further reason to respect the desires of its customers. It's why not having a moral system for decision making led the companies making and selling thalidomide, the Dalkon Shield, and asbestos to irresponsible actions.

The idea of responsibility—as shared, accountable decision making, if not as the full moral system for decision making described here—has led to deep changes and commitments at Saturn, Chemical Bank, Johnson & Johnson, Dayton Hudson Corporation, and many other organizations. What might the Responsibility System—as a moral attitude for value-based decision making—do for you?

## Finding Out About Yourself

Now, having thought about the following dilemmas in the previous chapter, look at them again in terms of the Responsibility System as an overall business attitude of mutual cooperation. Would your answers be any different now?

**Dilemma:** A strong prospect for computer sales manager comes before the executive selection committee for a final interview. You are chairperson of the committee. The candidate gives you a complete list of his current employer's clients, including their present system needs, their projected future needs, and recommended pricing.

1. Which of the Magnificent Seven apply to this situation?

    _____

    _____

    _____

    _____


2. When you consider responsibility as a moral attitude, which General Principle or Principles are most important in resolving the dilemma and defending your decision?

    _____

    _____

_____

_____

**Dilemma:** A company that produces defense munitions needs to test them. An uninhabited area that can be leased from the government is chosen as the test site. When plans for the tests are made public, a Native American tribe objects, claiming the land is an ancient and sacred burial ground. You must solve the problem.

1. Which of the Magnificent Seven apply to this situation?

   _____

   _____

   _____

   _____

2. When you consider responsibility as a moral attitude, which General Principle or Principles are most important in resolving the dilemma and defending your decision?

   _____

   _____

   _____

   _____

*8*

# Value-Based Decision Making

## The Three-Step Process

Now you are ready for the three-step value-based decision-making process itself. All the previous chapters have built toward this one; they have prepared you to learn and apply a new system for resolving organizational issues and dilemmas.

## How You Got Here

You looked first at the development of your own personal values and principles. Then you experienced some actual working principles that have been formed and used in organizations. Following that was a look at how differing values among stakeholders produce business dilemmas. Next, as a professional in the gray zone of business, you explored a new definition of ethics as a creative business skill for decision making. Then I presented two difficult but key notions: (1) how to see General Moral Principles represented in action options; and (2) how to rank options and their General Principles using the moral system of cooperative responsibility. All of that has readied you for the value-based decision-making process.

# Purpose of the Process

The three-step process has two purposes. One is to give you a practical means of merging business action options, working values and principles, and accepted General Moral Principles into a coherent picture. The other is to enable you to choose the best option for action more effectively, responsibly, and justifiably.

# How the Process Works

From a logical, step-by-step viewpoint, the process enables you to identify facts, stakeholders, their options and working principles, and outcomes, so as to clearly identify the dilemma. Then you can evaluate all the options for action by connecting them to the Magnificent Seven General Principles. At that point in the process, based on your prioritization of General Principles, you can choose the most "fitting" option for action.

The process does not guarantee you ready-made or perfect answers to a dilemma. It's far from a magic formula. But it does guide you toward the right questions. Recall that the skill of ethics is a matter of creating fitting answers to particular ethical situations. No process hands you the right answer any more than an ice skating coach can give you a national figure skating championship or a trainer can give you a management skill. *At the end of the decision-making process, you have to make the best choice you can from among several options and take action.*

### The Three-Step Process

1. *Examine the situation.*
   - Get the critical facts.
   - Identify the key stakeholders.
   - Identify each stakeholder's options (*what* each stakeholder wants done).
2. *Establish the dilemma.*
   - Identify the working principles and norms that drive each option (*why* each stakeholder wants it done).

- Project the possible outcomes (consequences) of each stakeholder option. Do any violate your principles, or those of your organization?
- Determine the actions (means) necessary to produce each outcome. Do any violate your principles, or those of your organization?
- State the dilemma.

3. *Evaluate the options.*
  - Identify the General Principle(s) behind each stakeholder option.
  - Compare the General Principle(s) behind each option. Which is the most responsible General Principle(s) in this situation?
  - The option with the most responsible General Principle(s) is your choice for action.

# A Case Study

Let's use an actual case to explain and demonstrate the three steps and their activities. Bob Zack is vice-president and general manager of the manufacturing division of SanCon, a successful, privately owned company that specializes in exterior glass panels for high-rise office buildings. Bob has a tough decision to make, and it's his call.

For some months, SanCon's CEO, Frank Williamson, and Bob's supervisors and peers have been pressuring him to replace his production manager, Pete Wolff, with a young, talented, experienced go-getter, Jim Ryan. Pete Wolff is fifty-one and a professional friend of Bob's; he has held his current position for twelve years and been with the company for thirty-one. Bob knows only too well that Pete's performance, long evaluated as "excellent," has begun to slip noticeably in the last two years, despite several discussions during performance review sessions followed by coaching.

Problems have arisen during the last year, when the company moved from full-authority foremen to a "team" and "team leader" management approach on the production floor. Also, line productivity has fallen somewhat, and the rejection rate at the quality control station has increased.

While Bob now agrees that a management change has to be made, his supervisors have pressured him to "just find a way to let this guy go quickly and get the show on the road" with Jim Ryan. The legal department, under general counsel Ted Hart, has a more specific plan in mind and is pushing it hard: (1) Assign Pete more projects and responsibilities than he can handle, (2) carefully document every incident of poor or mediocre performance for the next quarter, and (3) let Pete go after the quarterly performance review, giving him an early retirement deal if necessary. One object is not to let Pete build a case that could cause legal problems for SanCon.

Bob, as he thinks about it, has some problems with the pressure and the suggestions from the legal department. Pete is a longtime associate, has worked hard and well for many years, and has a family. Bob's natural management style would lead him to talk the situation over with Pete and, over the next few months, persuade him to resign, negotiate an early retirement, and help him plan his future. Bob knows that this could cause problems. With uneasiness, he begins to sense the dilemma; he knows it is his call to make.

# Step 1: Examine the Situation

The purpose of this step is simply to get the important facts of the situation. Your role is to be a researcher, putting subjective judgments on hold as much as possible. Generally speaking, a large percentage of problems can be solved within this step. Organizing the facts is often enough to point in the direction of a solution.

Emphasis is on getting the critical "givens" of the situation; formulating a picture of the whole problem; identifying all the important stakeholders with competing interests; and enumerating the possible options each stakeholder may want in this situation.

The specific activities in this step are:

1. *Get the critical facts.* What does the situation look like? What has happened? What are the circumstances involved?

2. *Identify the key stakeholders.* Who are the significant players? Include all the key stakeholders significantly affected by the situation and by any decisions you might make.

3. *Identify each stakeholder's options (what each stakeholder wants done).* As clearly as you can, state the options for action that represent each stakeholder's interest. Put yourself in the stakeholders' shoes and think from their point of view. This is not the time to make final judgments or slant stakeholder options from your own perspective.

## Application to the Case

Applying Step 1, Bob Zack collects the information. The pressure is on to let Pete Wolff go and hire Jim Ryan. Pete's performance has been slipping, and the company needs to improve its line productivity and quality.

Identifying the key players is not difficult for Bob. There's Pete and his family; Bob himself; Jim Ryan; Frank Williamson, CEO; Bob's supervisors and peers, who are essentially in agreement; and Ted Hart, general counsel. The lesser players are the team members under Pete Wolff.

As impartially as possible, since he himself is a key stakeholder, Bob identifies as best he can what each stakeholder's interest is—what each wants done in this situation.

| Stakeholders | Options |
| --- | --- |
| CEO | Change the management situation in production. |
| Supervisors and peers | Replace Wolff with Ryan. |
| Legal department | Replace Wolff by documenting poor performance. |
| Pete Wolff and family | Accede to termination; fight a known action; try to negotiate. |
| Jim Ryan | Accept or reject promotion. |
| Bob Zack | Use documentation method to replace Wolff, or use up-front communication and persuasion to retire Wolff. |

# Step 2: Establish the Dilemma

The purpose of this step is to clearly state the ethical dilemma present in the situation. As much as possible, you want to clarify the stakes, the interests, the arguments, and the options balanced on each side of the dilemma. At this point, it is key to see the whole picture, determine why others have different solutions, and not be narrowly tied to your own opinion as the only valid interest.

Your primary role in Step 2 is to put on the hat of an impartial observer. From your research in Step 1, you know what the salient facts of the situation are, who the major stakeholders are (including yourself), and what each stakeholder wants done in terms of options for action.

Now, with a vested interest in your own options, you must impartially look at *why* the other stakeholders want their options as a solution to the situation. You want to find out where they're coming from. This involves identifying stakeholders' working values, principles, and norms—the business reasons behind their options.

Then you project the possible outcomes or consequences of each stakeholder option and ask whether any violate your principles, or those of your organization. The answer ensures that options you consider for action flow from business principles acceptable to you and your organization.

You also want to look at the actions that stakeholders may take to gain their desired outcomes, because the actions necessary to an option are ethically important as means to an end. Some of those actions may, even at this point, violate your values and working principles, or those of the organization. You want to know now whether this is the case.

The specific activities of Step 2 are:

1. *Identify the working principles and norms that drive each option (why each stakeholder wants it done).* You want to pinpoint, as best you can, the business reasons for each option. Why is this stakeholder in favor of this option for action? The answers take the form of organizational or business working values and principles. The options show you what the stake-

holder values—sees as worthwhile—and the working principles that flow from those values.

2. *Project the possible outcomes (consequences) of each stakeholder option.* What will each stakeholder option cause to happen? What will be the result if a given option is followed? You are trying to discover what the stakeholder wants to have happen in this situation. Think as the stakeholder would think. Be objective. Then ask: *Do any of the outcomes resulting from these options violate my principles, or those of my organization?* That question is important. An option chosen for action must flow from accepted organizational values and principles. If it doesn't, then that option should not be considered as a valid choice for action.

3. *Determine the actions (means) necessary to produce each outcome.* What will stakeholders have to do to get the result they want? What steps will they take to make their desired options happen?

Then ask: *Do any of the actions they will take to make their options happen (means to the end) violate my principles, or those of my organization?* That question is important also. Not only is it necessary to choose an option with acceptable results, but the means or actions necessary to implement that option also have ethical implications. Generally, it is an accepted principle that "the end does not justify the means." Practically translated, this statement means that the result of an action (the end) must be ethical or principled, and so must the way that option is implemented (the means). We should not use unethical actions as means to make an ethical option happen. It might be fine to have a major business competitor out of the market. To get that competitor out through means that are illegal, unfair, or dishonest is usually neither valid, principled, nor fitting.

However, a caution is in order here. There are rare situations when the result (end) of an action is absolutely imperative but can be accomplished only by actions (means) that may be ethically questionable or unethical in themselves. It can be argued that if the means to the end are necessary, but of less importance and of less effect than the original purpose and result, they *may* be permitted. This kind of difficult ethical situation could well call for help from an ethics committee or a consultant or require a team approach.

Generally, if any of the stakeholder options demand implementation by actions that violate your principles, or those of your organization, then the option itself has to be seriously questioned.

4. *State the dilemma.* Through the activities completed, you know the stakeholders, the options they represent, the validity of the working principles behind their options, and the validity of the means to implement their options. You are now in a position to decide if what you are facing is a true dilemma (balanced opposite interests). You are now able to state, even write down, the dilemma exactly.

## Application to the Case

Applying the Step 2 activities to our case might look like this as Bob thinks through them:

### Identify the working principles and norms that drive each option.

| Stakeholders | Options | Working Principles and Norms |
|---|---|---|
| CEO | Change the management situation in production. | Improve productivity, quality control, and profit; implement "team" management. |
| Supervisors and peers | Replace Wolff with Ryan. | Same as CEO's values, plus promote good managers and replace poor ones; look out for company welfare. |
| Legal department | Replace Wolff by documenting poor performance. | Use quarterly review as means to replacement; further SanCon's business goals; avoid legal problems; serve as management resource; preserve legal department's own welfare. |
| Pete Wolff and family | Accede to termination; fight a known action; try to negotiate. | Protect career, keep job; care for family; fight if possible; don't burn bridges. |

| *Stakeholders* | *Options* | *Working Principles and Norms* |
|---|---|---|
| Jim Ryan | Accept or reject promotion. | Further career; do good work for SanCon. |
| Bob Zack | Use documenta-tion method to re-place Wolff. | Avoid legal problems; accomplish tasks well for SanCon; use company resources; protect job and career; promote fairness to other employees; avoid problems with supervisors. |
|  | *or* Use up-front com-munication and persuasion to re-tire Wolff. | *or* Accomplish tasks well for SanCon; avoid legal problems; promote fair-ness to others; protect career. |

**Project the possible outcomes (consequences) for each stakeholder option. Do any violate your principles or those of your organization?**

| *Stakeholders* | *Possible Outcomes* |
|---|---|
| CEO, supervisors, peers | All of these see the replacement of Wolff by Ryan. They see avoidance of legal problems through legal and accurate documentation of poor performance. Team management productivity will increase and quality control will improve—all adding to the bottom line. If legal action is taken, they're covered. |
| Legal department | Legal wants the same outcome as management. Wolff may catch on to why he is given more work; if so, he may begin to prepare his case. After Wolff is reviewed and let go, he may feel he has been unfairly treated and take legal action—but legal can handle it. |
| Pete Wolff and family | He may accede to replacement through an early retirement package. He may try to negotiate to stay on, but he will fail. He may take his case to court when replaced—but the company can handle it. |
| Jim Ryan | He will wait for termination to happen and then assume the position as manager of production, and he will do well. |

| Stakeholders | Possible Outcomes |
|---|---|
| Bob Zack | If I follow the documentation procedure, there will be a confrontation. We may reach an agreement on early retirement, or there may be an ensuing court case involving time and money. But Wolff will be replaced.<br>*or*<br>I can explain the situation, the company's intentions, Wolff's problems, and the need for change. I can offer him early retirement with outplacement help—but work *with* him for a satisfactory solution. Frank, supervisors, and peers will not favor this solution, but they will go along with it. |

Bob feels that none of the options' results violate his principles or SanCon's—replacing Pete Wolff is a valid result.

**Determine the actions (means) necessary to produce each outcome. Do any violate your principles or those of your organization?**

Here, Bob can pare down the stakeholder options. Williamson, the supervisors, and the peers have no concrete actions to take. They have made it clear what they want done and have told Bob to do it. To replace Wolff on productivity grounds does not violate company principles. In the minds of upper management, neither do the suggested means of accomplishing that goal. But Bob himself has questions: not about the ultimate result of the options, but about the means by which Pete Wolff is replaced. "Do the means to achieve this good end violate my own working principles?" thinks Bob. His application of this activity might resemble this:

| Stakeholder | Evaluation of Means |
|---|---|
| Legal department | Is the documentation procedure, though legal, really the best for me, SanCon, and Wolff? How will the other employees view it? Is a court case worth it? |
| Pete Wolff and family | Whatever actions Wolff may take in his own defense have no relation to my principles or those of the company, even though we might wish he would just accede to retirement. |

| *Stakeholder* | *Evaluation of Means* |
|---|---|
| Bob Zack | Both my options can bring about the desired result and do not violate company principles and norms. But I do have reservations about the documentation procedure, even if it's used to bring about a good result—Wolff's replacement. Does it violate my own sense of openness and fair play in terms of my relationship with Pete, the secrecy involved, and my own management style? And how will my other employees view me later? The option of working *with* Wolff, as a means to a good end, seems in keeping with my values and management style. But it risks a court case, disapproval from my manager and peers, and possible damage to my own career. |

**State the dilemma.**

For Bob, the dilemma is now clear. It is about the means, the actions, used to bring about the replacement of Wolff, not the end itself. Bob must decide to replace Wolff by (1) a documentation of poor performance procedure, which risks confrontation, possible legal proceedings, and possible ill will from his own employees; or (2) up-front communication, persuasion, and early retirement, which also risks court action and the disapproval of his own supervisors.

# Step 3: Evaluate the Options

Thus far, you have examined the situation: You have gathered the critical facts, identified the key stakeholders, and determined what they want done. You have also established the dilemma: You identified the working principles behind the stakeholders' options and projected the possible outcomes if those options were chosen.

The purpose of Step 3 is to help you choose one or more of the actions in an effort to resolve the dilemma you face. The guidelines, the touchstones, for your choice are the Magnificent Seven General Principles that drive possible options. Your role, once you have identified the General Principles behind the possible options, is judge and decision maker. And the reason for your choice of option or options is an ethical one—that one or more General Moral Principles are the most responsible in this situation. That reason also serves to justify your choice of options.

The specific activities of Step 3 are:

1. *Identify the General Principle(s) behind each stakeholder option.* Is this option driven primarily by dignity of human life, autonomy, honesty, loyalty, fairness, humaneness, or the common good? Or perhaps the option reflects several of the Magnificent Seven. The answer is not automatic or expedient; rather, it is a matter of honest judgment on your part. While you obviously can't read the mind and intentions of each stakeholder, here you want to assign the General Principle(s) that you genuinely think drives each possible option.

2. *Compare the General Principle(s) behind each option. Which is the most responsible General Principle(s) in this situation?* This is the time for the decision maker's "responsibility values check." In your mind, in this situation, which of the Magnificent Seven holds top priority as an ethical reason for this or that option? The object is to choose an option for action that represents the most responsible General Principle (or Principles) for you, now, in this situation.

As a result, you will have a truly "principled" decision for action. With an attitude of responsibility, autonomy may hold a higher priority than loyalty for you, now, in this situation. Or the common good may outweigh fairness to one individual, not in general, but here and now. An option may represent several General Principles; this is often a clue to the option's importance.

This activity is a judgment call on your part—in fact, it is the key activity in your decision-making process. There is no set call, no sure answer, and no guarantee of universal agreement on the part of others. There is no process for a ready-made and perfect answer here. It is your call and your responsibility. Ethics is not finding out what the correct moral decision is. Ethics is making, fashioning, creating a moral decision for action.

3. *The option with the most responsible General Principle(s) is your choice for action.* Your decision is not a guess, a choice from ignorance, or a choice from expediency. It is a

choice for action derived from principles. And it is a decision that is defensible on the grounds of principle and an attitude of cooperative responsibility.

## *Two Potential Problems*

What if you, as the decision maker faced with a dilemma, find your personal business/ethical principles in conflict with those of your organization? Sometime it's going to happen—to you. That conflict has to be resolved first. It also involves the relative importance of the Magnificent Seven as you interpret them. Does autonomy (here, your own self-interest) outweigh loyalty to the organization and perhaps the common good of many? Are the means to an end indefensible, although the results of an action are good? Is it possible to find another option that serves your personal moral imperatives as well as the interests others have?

Is the conflict or its frequency so serious that more fundamental questions about your work situation must be addressed? Perhaps you need to rethink your own principles in order to be more sure of them. Perhaps certain organizational principles need change or clarification. Personal and organizational values can and do change, but not for the sake of expediency. These difficult but realistic questions must be solved or somehow reconciled for you to proceed with your solution to the dilemma.

Here's another potential difficulty. Let's say you have followed all the steps and activities down to choosing the most responsible General Principle or Principles behind possible options. But no one principle or group of principles stands out as an indication of which option to choose. They themselves seem balanced in number and responsibility. What do you do then? First, look again to see if an option you have is in fact legitimately driven by more General Principles than you first thought. If so, that option may be a very fitting answer. Second, look for the possibility of choosing several options that, when taken together, may be a fitting solution.

## *Application to the Case*

Applying the activities of Step 3 to our case might look like this for Bob:

**Identify the General Principle(s) behind each stakeholder option.**

1. *Dignity of human life.* The lives of people are to be respected.
2. *Autonomy.* All persons, including ourselves, are intrinsically valuable and have the right to self-determination.
3. *Honesty.* The truth should be told to those who have a right to know it.
4. *Loyalty.* Promises, contracts, and commitments should be honored.
5. *Fairness.* People should be treated justly.
6. *Humaneness.* Our actions ought to accomplish good. They should avoid evil. They should be of benefit to others and ourselves.
7. *The common good.* Actions should accomplish the "greatest good for the greatest number" of people.

Looking at each option for action, Bob identifies which General Principle or Principles, if any, drive each option under consideration:

CEO (autonomy, common good)

Frank Williamson has made it clear that he wants Wolff out and Ryan in. He values greater profit through increased productivity, better quality control, and a new team management approach (autonomy and common good).

Supervisors and peers (loyalty, autonomy)

They want the same results as Frank. They want to see good managers promoted and poor ones replaced. Such actions signal a reward for good service (loyalty), which is also in their own interests (autonomy).

Legal department (autonomy, loyalty, fairness)

Ted Hart has made legal's case. He certainly wants to further SanCon's business goals and help management to achieve them (autonomy, loyalty). Ted also wants to document Pete's poor performance as proof for removal. This recommendation, I am sure, is not made out of malice but simply perceived as an effective, legal way to effect change, covering the company in case of a suit (fairness).

| | |
|---|---|
| Pete Wolff and family (autonomy, common good, honesty) | Pete wants to keep his job, protect his career, or at least make a deal without burning bridges (autonomy). He intends to do the best for his family (common good). If forced to, Pete may fight for his job (autonomy), but he probably expects me to be open and truthful with him (honesty). |
| Jim Ryan (autonomy, loyalty) | Jim expects to advance his career (autonomy) and do good work for SanCon (loyalty). |
| Bob Zack (loyalty, autonomy, fairness, humaneness, honesty) | If I were to choose the documentation method for replacing Wolff, I would want to accomplish the task well for SanCon, avoid legal problems, and use company resources such as legal (loyalty). I would want an employee treated justly under company policy and principles (fairness) and would want to protect my own job, career, and reputation (autonomy). *or* With the up-front approach, I would accomplish my task for the company while trying to avoid legal problems (loyalty). Again, I would want to protect my job and career (autonomy) while being just and open with a longtime colleague (fairness, humaneness, honesty). |

When Bob is done, he has a chart that clearly establishes each stakeholder's options, his or her working principles, and the General Principles that drive them.

| Stakeholders | Options | Working Principles and Norms | General Principles |
|---|---|---|---|
| CEO | Change the management situation in production. | Improve productivity, quality control, and profit; implement "team" management. | Autonomy and common good |
| Supervisors and peers | Replace Wolff with Ryan. | Same as CEO's values, plus promote good managers and replace poor ones; look out for company welfare. | Loyalty and autonomy |

| Stakeholders | Options | Working Principles and Norms | General Principles |
|---|---|---|---|
| Legal department | Replace Wolff by documenting poor performance. | Use quarterly review as means to replacement; further SanCon's business goals; avoid legal problems; serve as management resource; preserve legal department's own welfare. | Autonomy, loyalty, and fairness |
| Pete Wolff and family | Accede to termination; fight a known action; try to negotiate. | Protect career, keep job; care for family; fight if possible; don't burn bridges. | Autonomy, common good, and honesty |
| Jim Ryan | Accept or reject promotion. | Further career; do good work for SanCon. | Autonomy and loyalty |
| Bob Zack | Use documentation method to replace Wolff. | Avoid legal problems; accomplish tasks well for SanCon; use company resources; protect job and career; promote fairness to other employees; avoid problems with supervisors. | Loyalty, autonomy, and fairness |
| | *or* Use up-front communication and persuasion to retire Wolff. | *or* Accomplish tasks well for SanCon; avoid legal problems; promote fairness to others; protect career. | Honesty, loyalty, fairness, humaneness, and autonomy |

## Compare the General Principles behind each option.

Which is the most responsible General Principle(s) in this situation? Bob now completes the decision-making process with his own "responsibility values check" on the General Principles identified.

It is clear to him that the purpose of the options is shared by all the stakeholders except Wolff. While all the General Principles are important, autonomy, the common good, and loyalty seem the most responsible to SanCon's upper management.

Bob's real dilemma is with the means taken to replace Wolff. Is the documentation method fair, humane, and honest to Wolff? And does it really serve the autonomy and the common good of SanCon, especially when viewed by others outside of the managers? It would certainly accomplish the immediate purpose and please upper management. Is it truly responsible?

Could the same result be accomplished by Bob's other option and still serve loyalty, autonomy, fairness, and the common good of all concerned? As he thinks about it, Bob wonders if his second option, which emphasizes humaneness and honesty, could get the job done once and for all, even if it risks a court case and the possible displeasure of his supervisors. It is Bob's call alone. Which principle or principles are the most responsible now, in this situation?

**The option with the most responsible General Principle(s) is your choice for action.**

The decision maker chooses an option after carefully considering the stakes, the options, and the General Principles of the important stakeholders involved, including his or her own. The decision reflects an action option chosen on principle and from an attitude of responsibility. Precisely because it encompasses working values, principles, the Universal General Principles, and an attitude of responsible cooperation, the decision for action is defensible—its moral reasoning helps justify the actions taken.

Bob Zack's decision will be the most "fitting" he can create. It will not be a perfect decision, it may have troublesome side effects, and it will be challenged by others. Bob knows, though, that it will be the best he can do, here and now. "That's the often complicated life of a decision maker," Bob tells himself—and you.

And what of Bob's solution? I have posed this real case, not uncommon in organizational life, as a demonstration of the value-based decision-making process. I leave you with a final question: How would you decide this dilemma if you were Bob?

# Finding Out About Yourself

Practice makes better, not perfect. I suggest you put the total three-step process into practice for the first time right now. But this first time, I want you to use the following chart pages as you apply the steps and activities. Also, I want you to choose your own dilemma; it will make the exercise up close and personal for you.

## The Decision-Making Process

*Step 1: Examine the Situation*

- Get the critical facts.
- Identify the key stakeholders.
- Identify each stakeholder's options (*what* each stakeholder wants done).

*Step 2: Establish the Dilemma*

- Identify the working principles and norms that drive each option (*why* each stakeholder wants it done).
- Project the possible outcomes (consequences) of each stakeholder option. Do any violate your principles, or those of your organization?
- Determine the actions (means) necessary to produce each outcome. Do any violate your principles, or those of your organization?
- State the dilemma.

*Step 3: Evaluate the Options*

- Identify the General Principle(s) behind each stakeholder option.
- Compare the General Principle(s) behind each option. Which is the most responsible General Principle(s) in this situation?
- The option with the most responsible General Principle(s) is your choice for action.

## The Magnificent Seven Universal General Principles

1. *Dignity of human life:* The lives of persons are to be respected. Example: not intending or doing harm to others.

2. *Autonomy: All persons, including ourselves, are intrinsically valuable and have a right to self-determination.* Examples: acting in ways that demonstrate each person's worth; acting for one's own legitimate needs.

3. *Honesty: The truth should be told to those who have a right to know it.* Examples: speaking and acting in ways that reflect the way things are in reality.

4. *Loyalty: Promises, contracts, and commitments should be honored.* Examples: honoring confidentiality and keeping proprietary information secret; honoring written and oral contracts; doing what one says one will do.

5. *Fairness: People should be treated justly.* Examples: one's right to life's necessities and the duty to ensure them for others; the right of all to fair treatment under work contracts, company policies, and the law; duty to help those in deep need, those in danger, and those who are helpless.

6. *Humaneness: (1) Our actions should accomplish good; (2) our actions should avoid evil. Actions should be of benefit to ourselves and others.* Examples: performing good acts, not evil ones; acting and speaking so as to be of benefit to others; acting and speaking in ways that benefit one's own valid self-interest.

7. *The common good: Actions should accomplish the "greatest good for the greatest number" of people.* Examples: speaking and acting, whenever possible, for the welfare of the most people, as long as individual rights are not violated.

## Step 1: Examine the Situation

- Get the critical facts.
- Identify the key stakeholders.
- Identify each stakeholder's options (*what* each stakeholder wants done).

| |
|---|
| Critical Facts: |
| |
| |
| |
| |
| |
| |
| |
| Stakeholders: |
| 1. |
| 2. |
| 3. |
| 4. |
| 5. You, as decision maker |

## Identify Stakeholder Options:

| 1. Stakeholder Options: | 2. Stakeholder Options: |
|---|---|
|  |  |

| 5. My Options: |
|---|
|  |

| 3. Stakeholder Options: | 4. Stakeholder Options: |
|---|---|
|  |  |

## Step 2: Establish the Dilemma

- Identify the working principles and norms that drive each option (*why* each stakeholder wants it done).
- Project the possible outcomes (consequences, results) of each stakeholder option. Do any violate your principles, or those of your organization?
- Determine the actions (means) necessary to produce each outcome. Do any violate your principles, or those of your organization?
- State the dilemma.

| Options | Working Principles and Norms | Consequences (Results) | OK or not? | Actions as Means to Results (OK or not?) |
|---------|------------------------------|------------------------|------------|------------------------------------------|
|         |                              |                        |            |                                          |

The dilemma is:

_____ vs._____

## Step 3: Evaluate the Options

- Identify the General Principle(s) behind each option.
- Compare the General Principle(s) behind each option. Which is the most responsible General Principle(s) in this situation?
- The option with the most responsible General Principle(s) is your choice for action.

| Options | General Principles | Comparison of General Principles ("Responsibility Values Check") | Choice of Priority General Principle(s) |
|---|---|---|---|
| | | | |

My option for action is:

_____

_____

_____

# 9

# Differences as Opportunities

## Adapting Decisions to a Global Marketplace

The past few years have yielded exciting new international business opportunities for organizations. Political and economic changes in Eastern Europe, the Middle East, and Africa have opened new vistas for commerce, services, and investment. The revolutionary activities within the USSR and the Balkan countries are recent examples. And the near future will see many more possibilities—and difficult challenges.

While new realities beckon, cultures often clash. The old, familiar, frustrating issues of human interaction still remain: deep differences in values, customs, traditions, ways of living, and therefore ways of doing business. With the new opportunities come old problems.

## Questions for Today

How can you respond better to new opportunities despite existing cultural and ethical differences among peoples? How can often conflicting business and ethical systems result in more mutually successful business transactions? This chapter explores those questions in the context of value-based decision making.

## The Scope of the Challenge

A smaller planet has put varied nations and peoples face-to-face as never before. Only now are we coming to grips with how different yet intertwined our histories, cultures, customs, lives, and values really are. They are as different yet proximate as camels loping by Abrams tanks in the desert; mud-and-thatch huts only minutes away from million-dollar suburban homes; Native Americans making silent decisions in a kiva, while nearby corporate boards argue policies in skyscrapers; or foreign nationals graduating from Harvard Business School and returning to villages in Yemen, Nigeria, or Panama, while their American counterparts interview for Xerox and Citicorp in Manhattan.

Consider more concrete examples of cultural and ethical differences among countries. In parts of Africa, a "family" celebration at the conclusion of a business deal—a party for which you are asked to pay—may well be a sign of friendship and lasting business relationships, not a personal payoff. "Grease payments" to customs officials in some countries may be part of their earning a living wage—not necessarily blackmail. In a large number of countries, custom, law, and religion support the fact that women are denied personal and professional rights of equality. Payment of a large sum to a Filipino or Korean government official in order to get a contract over the competition is often an outright personal payoff—sanctioned or not by local law and custom. Each of these practices is part of some group's ethical standards and affects business dealings between you and the group's members.

The problem is one of differences—a conflict of values, principles, and norms among stakeholders—but not necessarily of right versus wrong, truth against falsehood, or knowledge encountering ignorance. It is certainly not a question of our "good ethics" versus their "bad ethics." Such a view begs the integrity question, but more importantly, it risks destroying any sense of cooperation based on mutual trust and goodwill.

The real challenge is to bridge differences, value gaps, judgments, suspicions, and your own perceived obstacles. In today's world, there is much to be accomplished and mutually gained. The opportunities are there, but so is the clash of values and interests.

## The Magnificent Seven Revisited

The differences among us are certainly real enough, even though we all share the same human nature and the same small planet. Even the most universal, commonly held principles of human behavior among peoples—the Magnificent Seven—are interpreted differently in various other countries and cultures. These differences affect your decision making and the outcomes of business transactions.

Let's look at a small sampling of conflicting values and the questions they raise for organizations in the context of the seven Universal General Principles—the most common moral denominators people share in making decisions.

1. *Dignity of human life*. The value and dignity of human life varies from country to country around the world. Whatever the reasons, life is more valued and protected in some countries than in others. This fact becomes apparent when business is conducted. Some countries allow the "dumping" of medicines, food, and other products deemed unsafe, or not safe enough, into other countries. Countries sell sophisticated weapons, even illegally, to nations that have used them—or will use them—on the selling nation itself or its allies. We have witnessed in recent years the sanctioned starvation of thousands of a country's population for narrow political purposes.

These are serious moral as well as business issues, and they give rise to hard questions. What about countries that publicly hold strong dignity-of-human-life values but don't practice them? Are these realities of practical concern to organizations? What are the rights and obligations of organizations that directly or indirectly contribute to such actions? What rights and obligations must be faced by the buying nations themselves?

2. *Autonomy*. The right to self-determination is the keystone of democracy in the United States, but not so everywhere in the world. Are investments in South Africa under apartheid,

or arms sales to oppressive dictatorships, "not our problem"? Shouldn't we have the income, since countries "will buy them from someone anyway"? Americans have extensive protection-of-privacy rights not even considered in many other countries. How do companies deal with that difference in values when foreign business affects individual rights?

The differences in values even extend to choice of social manners. Formality, touching, personal space, and signs of affection vary widely among nationalities and countries. They even influence business dealings; so how do we handle social amenities? In the majority of African countries, women do not inherit land, are not encouraged to attend school, perform the hard manual labor, and have little if any means of controlling conception. In Uganda, the Women's Lawyers Association recently began a campaign that attempted to convince women that wife battering is not a sign of a man's love. How do our gender values influence dealings with African nations?

How is freedom of choice honored by both buyer and seller stakeholder countries? American organizations usually cannot and should not attempt to change the ways other countries live and do business. But where does direct or tacit approval of oppression in order to do business begin and end? Do you have any responsibility to freedom of choice in other countries— responsibility that can be reflected in business decisions?

3. *Honesty.* Immense differences concerning honor and integrity exist around the world, and the interpretation of what honesty means differs even among ethnic groups in the United States. What some may call dishonesty is often deeply ingrained in the cultures of other peoples and viewed as a normal, ethical, acceptable, and necessary way of living and working.

Questions and problems in the area of honesty resulted in a significant and controversial piece of legislation: the Foreign Corrupt Practices Act of 1977 (FCPA). It is a prime example of a legislative reaction to dilemmas over differences in basic values. Bribing of foreign officials, parties, or candidates (prohibited under the FCPA) is a normal and even valued way of doing business in some countries. In fact, failure to make elaborate gifts can be taken as a serious personal insult in some societies, rather than as an attempt by companies to be honest.

The FCPA distinction between "public officials" and those whose duties are "essentially ministerial and clerical" is helpful, but the larger problems of doing business—given restrictive laws, customs, cultures, and values—remain. Is calling a company's "agents" (whose actions are attributable to the employer) "independent distributors" (which breaks the causation chain) an ethical answer or just a legalistic maneuver?

4. *Loyalty and fairness.* The fulfillment of promises, contracts, and commitments in a context of justice is variously interpreted around the world. The world of commerce (as viewed in Western nations) can be solid ground in some countries, but a quicksand of changing alliances, broken contracts, political power, lying, and injustice in others. In many countries, price fixing, privileged people, powerful companies, and government corruption contrast sharply with U.S. antitrust policies. Significant U.S. legal restrictions on business embody American values and ethics. Even the U.S. Tax Code is aimed at a redistribution of wealth based on discernible values. Antitrust, price-fixing, and insider-trading rules arise from an American sense of fairness, as do laws prohibiting discrimination in employment. Rights of the individual, including privacy, freedom of information, and due process, flow from the U.S. Constitution and Bill of Rights.

What is the effect on your decision making when these legally expressed values have low priority or do not exist in another culture? Does it matter that the legal expression is simply lacking? Is there a difference if the value is "not there," or if it is just given a different priority than in the United States?

There are many instances of "difficulty" in doing business in Japan, where priorities of respect and truthfulness are clearly different from those in the United States. An important U.S. contract with two Japanese entities nearly unraveled when the second Japanese company voiced a complaint over the excessive profits taken by the first company. In the United States the emphasis would have been on the amount of the profits; the Japanese issue was not the amount, but the misleading explanation given by the first company. Yet despite the high emphasis on truthfulness, it is the custom in Japan to strenuously avoid the word *no*. To ask a direct question (a given in American negotiation) is an offense.

A U.S. tax lawyer in France is told by a resident that "no one pays taxes here" and that an effort to comply with tax laws is frowned upon. An Italian company is deliberately not registered with its tax authority—not an uncommon practice, according to an Italian businessperson. A French management consultant criticizes a French bank for employing women as managers in branches dealing with Third World countries. Need an American company have concerns about these instances?

And what about the fairness issues involved in U.S. prohibitions against discrimination? A large American company recently told a woman in top management that it could not promote her to the next position because the job required doing business with Japan. A major media company had a woman travel in an Arab country, where she was arrested because she was alone. Is the message of "effectiveness" more important than the message of fairness?

5. *Humaneness*. This principle does not apply to large parts of world society, at least as we tend to interpret its two principles of accomplishing good and avoiding evil. The Iraqi and Kuwaiti treatment of prisoners and captured civilians, contrasted with such treatment by the coalition forces in the Gulf War, comes to mind. Amnesty International's reports on detention and torture around the globe chill the heart. Hatred and revenge toward longtime enemies flourish between various nations and peoples; some are among the wealthy and industrialized countries. Oppression of millions of people by powerful dictators, governments, and business cartels is still the rule in many parts of the world, making a mockery of care, compassion, and sharing— the hallmarks of humaneness.

Do you and your organization, which conducts business around the world, have responsibility *to* (if not *for*) any of these situations? If so, what are your responsibilities? And since when are the organizational and governmental histories of developed nations—the United States, Great Britain, France, Italy, Israel, the Soviet Union, and others—above reproach?

Some authorities argue that any acceptance of social responsibility beyond making money for shareholders undermines free society. Others hold that since the economic and social effects of major decisions cannot be separated, business is part of the social system. Which is it?

6. *The common good.* "The greatest good for the greatest number" has always seemed to evade the reach of human beings, who are continually caught between the natural pull of self-interest and its demand to also ensure the welfare of others.

The widening gap between the rich and the poor in most countries is a stark and frightening example of the unrealized "common good of the many." It is one of the most threatening economic, social, and moral factors at work today. It insulates the affluent from having to fully live the Magnificent Seven Principles; it forces the poor into a "survival ethic" that permits anything to avoid a living hell. Are there ethical/business policies you and other organizations should effect, thereby contributing to change for the good of both people and business?

Environmental issues and the common good are now at a point of urgency. Preservation of the earth is perhaps the most pressing moral and business issue. We have witnessed what warring people can do to our common, fragile planet in the skies over Kuwait and in the Persian Gulf waters. The damage to the air and sea is only one more incident of violence to our common thread of life—and, I'm sure, there's more to come. It can be argued from an ethical and responsibility perspective that no nation or organization has exclusive rights over the delicate ecosystem we call earth. Our planet is one interrelated whole; its integrity is absolutely necessary for each and all of us to survive. Is any person, nation, or organization morally free to devastate it for any reason?

> "The earth does not belong to man, man belongs to the earth. . . . Man did not weave the web of life, he is merely a strand in it. Whatever he does to the web, he does to himself."
> —Chief Seattle, in his reply to the U.S. government (c. 1852)

I sense that, within the framework of changing and emerging world values, one of the accepted ethical traditions will soon be overturned: humankind's superior importance over natural things, which have always been at its service and whim. The day is not too far off when a serious, intentional act of environmental degradation by a nation or organization will be considered a crime equal to or greater than direct violence to people. And the justifying reason will be that the welfare of a number of individual human beings is less important than the integrity of the environment. The argument will use the principle of common survival for all versus the selfish actions of a few.

But what should your role, and the roles of organizations, be when the common good demands actions seemingly beyond your welfare and that of organizations themselves? Are the issues of the gap between rich and poor and the integrity of the environment in any way the responsibility of those of us active in the global marketplace? Is the common good of many a positive business opportunity, rather than just an insurmountable or irrelevant social obstacle?

Given these samples of realities, conflicts of values, and questions cast in the setting of General Moral Principles, what practical answers are possible for you and other organizational decision makers? Can differing social, moral, economic, and business value systems be reconciled for mutual benefit?

## Suggestions for Organizational Action

### Two Initial Questions

A basic step in finding practical solutions to your problems and challenges in a global market is to answer two initial questions. First, do you accept the premise that most decisions are both business and ethical in nature? Second, are you an American businessperson or member of an organization that happens to do business overseas, or are you a global businessperson or member of an organization that happens to have headquarters in the United States?

Your answer to the first question embodies a key philosophical commitment. An affirmative answer means adoption of primary working values and principles—like the health and welfare of customers—from which action decisions will be made. Your answer to the second question determines a key responsibility commitment; it makes other countries and peoples either valued stakeholder partners or just potential profit centers and resource sites.

## Awareness of Stakeholder Viewpoints

Another step toward better global decision making is to be aware of, and acknowledge, the clash among different cultures, customs, values, and principles. This acknowledgment is really a process of learning about other cultures without making business or moral judgments based solely on American customs and mores. You should know the historical, ethnic, cultural, political, legal, and religious facts about a country or region, as these facts influence the way the people think, interact, and do business. And then you should allow those facts to affect your thinking and acting.

Acknowledgment of the differences should also include a tolerance of diversity. Our values, beliefs, customs, and ethics are not the only acceptable and correct ones. Many nations have value systems that did not evolve from Graeco-Roman and Anglo-Saxon roots, which emphasize the rule of law. Americans easily forget how relatively young and unique the Constitution and Bill of Rights are. Most other systems were practiced for centuries before the United States existed. The values and customs of other nations are not necessarily primitive, degraded, or wrong because ours are different. Hence, they don't call for our immediate suspicion, distrust, or condemnation. Until proved otherwise, they are only different—having evolved under other geographies, conditions, demands, and heritages.

By way of example, let's look at the practical problems of bribery and payoffs. Most foreign governments, including many well-known for corruption, have enforced statutes against most forms of private payoff. In Malaysia, bribery is publicly frowned on and punishable by imprisonment. In the Soviet Union, officials who solicit bribes can be executed. Yet in some countries of Africa, ancient traditions take precedence over law. Payoffs have become the norm and are rooted in a "communal heritage," in which a community leader's wealth was shared with the community; those who hoarded were scorned. The Nigerian practice of *dash*—private pay for private service—traces back to trade in the form of gifts exchanged for labor. Today, businesspeople of undeveloped nations who deal with the developed countries have not forgotten their communal obligations. Americans unfamiliar with communal nuances tend to sense cultural and ethical dilemmas, and they may judge foreign colleagues as unethical and corrupt. That verdict may be true by American standards but not by theirs.

American organizations frequently deal through foreign nationals who have been educated in the United States, know American business ways, but are very much a part of their own culture. They may hold seemingly conflicting values: some instilled in the West, others a part of their local tradition and life. They may see no conflict in negotiating along Western lines and then reverting to communal traditions when discussing more private remuneration. They need not be labeled completely corrupt; rather, they are drawn by both indigenous and Western values. They may have American ideals of personal business enrichment and want to adhere to communal obligations at the same time. Requests for payoffs may come from either value.

If you are involved in the Third World, you also need to learn about three ancient traditions that affect business transactions and added remuneration: the inner circle, future favors, and the gift exchange.[1]

Communal societies divide people into two groups: those with whom they have relationships, and those with whom they have none—the goal being group prosperity and protection. There are the "in" people and the "out" people; the "ins" are family, the others strangers. In East and West Africa, inner circles can be true relatives, comrades, or persons of similar age or region. In China, they may be those who share the same dialect; in India, members of the same caste. They are not unlike the "old boy networks" in the United States. The effect in many of these countries is to restrict social and business dealings to those with whom they have safe relationships. All others inspire fear simply because they are unknown. Indeed, some non-Western businesspeople prefer to deal only with those they know and trust. Often that trust is forthcoming if Westerners willing to honor communal values become part of the inner circle.

The system of future favors operates within the inner circles. In Japan it is known as "inner duty," in Kenya "inner relationship," and in the Philippines "inner debt." In these traditions, the person obligated to another is expected to repay the favor sometime in the future. Some form of favor or service will repay the earlier debt; this repayment then places the grantor of the original favor under future obligation. Lifelong, shifting, mutual obligations create relationships of trust and are the basis for doing business.

In many non-Western circles, the gift exchange tradition has evolved into a business tool: Gifts begin a process of future favors. They are an immediate sign of gratitude or hospitality, and they bring pleasure, but upon acceptance, they generate an obligation that the recipient must someday repay. In Moslem areas of Africa and Asia, food and drink are followed by buying, followed by a larger gift during the next visit, which generates a still larger purchase. The purpose is not only merchandising, but also a deepening and unending relationship that enriches both parties.

Inner circles, future favors, and gift exchanges exist in American society also, but they don't usually have the same sense of obligation—either in the present or in the future. Nor is there the same sense of "family" with ensuing trust or loyalty present. Rather, many Americans feel a sense of ethical wariness when the relationship seems to move beyond gratitude, courtesy, or friendliness to even remotely suggest influence in decision making.

## Working With Your Principles—and Theirs

Awareness and acknowledgment of differences in values among regions should bring about changes in your thinking and initiatives.

Practices you view as questionable, illegal, or simply exploitive may be revealed as local tradition, courtesy, and even friendship. I'm not suggesting that you break or ignore your own country's laws or those of other nations. Nor am I condoning outright begging, blackmail, or bribery. They spell financial, legal, and ethical trouble for you, your organization, and possibly those of other countries. But you can take initiatives other than outright rejection of legitimate values different from yours on the one hand, or completely selling out your own values on the other.

You can capitalize on new and existing opportunities for business in the following general ways:

1. Become more sensitive to the customs, values, and practices of other peoples, which they themselves view as moral, traditional, practical, and effective.
2. Don't judge the business customs of others—when different from your own—as necessarily immoral, corrupt, primitive, dangerous, or unworkable. Take them as legitimate and workable until proved otherwise.
3. Find legitimate ways to operate from *their* ethical and commercial points of view; do not demand that they operate only by your ground rules.
4. Avoid rationalizing borderline actions, which are usually justified by the following:
   • "This isn't 'really' illegal or immoral."
   • "This is in the organization's and my best interest."
   • "We're safe; no one will find out."
   • "The organization will condone this and protect me."
5. Refuse to do business when stakeholder options violate or seriously compromise laws, fundamental organizational values, or the Magnificent Seven Principles as you understand them.
6. Conduct relationships, negotiations, and agreements as openly and aboveboard as possible—including reports to stakeholders and public accountability.
7. Avoid purely legalistic but ethically questionable strategies, such as calling "agents" (who are accountable to employers) "distributors" (who are not).

## The Results System

Looking closely at the results or consequences of foreign practices rather than the actions themselves can clarify difficult situations. Gift giving is a good example. Solicitation of gifts has no place in U.S. business circles when it smacks of exploitation. This may be true in other countries too, but foreign colleagues are often at a loss as to how to initiate honorable, lasting relationships that form around business ventures—especially when Americans have little time for social amenities, are ignorant of local traditions, and are wary of the exchange of gifts that creates obligations and trust. Foreigners often take on the role of initial giver or suggest that gift giving is the traditional way of entering the local business system. These roles are viewed as a courteous and acceptable means of furthering business. You should look at the true purpose and legitimate consequences of such gift giving, considered in a local context other than your own.

An American company that exclusively manufactured and distributed medical devices for human implantation was asked for payment outside the contract; if it did not comply, it would lose the right to sell in a certain foreign country. The company had to weigh payment to certain nongovernmental parties against the life-and-death need of hundreds of citizens who could not obtain the device by any other means. Weighing the good consequences of an action against a questionably ethical "means to the end" makes for a tough call. A decision for remuneration in some form could well be the right one, given the importance of the devices versus an unwanted but unavoidable payment. The Magnificent Seven Principles (the common good of many and humane consequences) come into play as possible justifying ethical reasons. You may have situations like that.

> "Every organization has, and must have, ethics. This ethics, if acknowledged, helps the organization learn quickly and adapt to a complex, changing world."
> —Mark Pastin, ethicist and author

## The Responsibility System

A promise to respond to important stakeholders in a spirit of cooperation that fosters goodwill also allows for new initiatives in doing business in foreign countries. Whereas directly granting requests for private monies exposes U.S. organizations to financial and legal threats, invoking the principle of responsibility *to*—but not *for*—other stakeholders makes alternate answers appropriate. Nonmonetary public service benefits could well replace payoffs and satisfy the needs of both sides.

I wonder if the spectre of foreign payoffs and bribes doesn't sometimes blind American organizations to the fact that technical expertise, follow-up satisfaction, and customer service are also powerful incentives to buy. Responsibility to the customer through quality, partnering, and service is the name of the game today. It has top priority within the United States—why not overseas as well?

Foreigners love their countries as keenly as you do your own, and they want to see conditions improve. While firmly rejecting direct private payoffs, you may counter with monies clearly and openly directed at needed help to others not touched by the contracts themselves. Even if these funds make the foreign contacts richer, in the long run some portion of the wealth is often shared communally with many kin, relatives, and "mates." In fact, Kenya and Indonesia have made such requests of U.S. companies. It is not uncommon for non-Westerners to view requests for private monies as a way of helping themselves, but also as a means to aid larger groups and their nations.

Responsibility can also suggest that donations—in funds or materials roughly equal to the amount requested privately— could be open contributions to build or run schools, hospitals, rural medical clinics, or agricultural projects. Such donations could be directed to the provinces or villages of the foreign counterparts or colleagues. Donating service, tools, or machine parts is another alternative to private payoffs. Tanzanian wild-life-poaching patrols have been helped in this way by British companies, and Coca-Cola hired Egyptians to plant acres of orange trees. Both cases resulted in needed political favor, increased local employment, and goodwill.

The object, of course, is self-interest on both sides. But cooperation and goodwill are the responsible means. Public service, donations, prestige, employment, social progress, and the use of local customs and traditions are valid enough. They are far superior to bribes, insult, misunderstanding, or simply walking away from mutual business opportunity and benefit.

The FCPA prohibits payments to foreign officials, political parties, or candidates for the purpose of influencing an act or decision intended to obtain or retain business. Companies and their managers are also liable if they know or had reason to know that their agents used payments from a U.S. concern to pay foreign officials for a prohibited purpose. Nowhere does the FCPA prohibit the use of funds to aid developing societies.

You and organizations can often solve ethical/business dilemmas by turning private payoffs into public services. By doing so, you meet the organizational and ethical standards of the Responsibility System. Such decisions would then be openly defensible and justifiable on ethical as well as legal grounds—a powerful argument.

## The Three-Step Decision-Making Process

Ultimately, you will want to apply the three-step process to issues or dilemmas posed in the global marketplace.

1. *Examine the situation.* Acknowledgment of the histories, customs, and values of the peoples involved gives added insight into the critical facts of the situation. You are able to identify the key stakeholders, who may be more numerous than in the United States. Communal traditions, inner circle relationships, and non-Western colleagues lengthen the list. All of them may have significant interests in the business opportunity. Stakeholder options are more easily and clearly identified, given your new awareness of what the stakeholders want done.

2. *Establish the dilemma.* Identifying the working principles and norms that drive each of the stakeholder options (why they want their options chosen) is more predictable using the decision-making process. Since foreign values and principles are likely to differ from those you quickly and accurately assign to American clients, the issue or dilemma in the situation is more focused and accurate than before.

With a more balanced acknowledgment of why foreigners hold certain values and "stakes" when approaching business, you won't need to be so negatively judgmental of their intentions. Projecting the outcomes of the stakeholders' options should then be closer to reality and less colored by your own values and principles. Remember that these first two steps, up to this point, are meant to be completed primarily in the role of researcher and fact finder, not judge.

Then you can attempt to determine the actions that stakeholders will take to produce the outcome they want. At this point, you ask whether those actions, as means to the end, violate your own or organizational principles. Going beyond awareness and acknowledgment, you may see significant clashes of your values, your principles, organizational principles, and laws with theirs. But now you can see common values you both share. Awareness of their values and customs helps you to judge more accurately and fairly whether the means they will use in fulfillment of their options are acceptable or unacceptable ground rules for you as well. And then you are able to state the issue or dilemma as it exists.

3. *Evaluate the options.* The key to value-based decision making is to choose an option for action that flows from business values and principles rooted responsibly in the Magnificent Seven General Principles. Given your awareness of the similarities and differences in interpretation of General Principles by other peoples, attempt to identify which Principle(s) is driving each stakeholder option, including your own. Your understanding of how and why the people of other countries think and act as they do is deeper than before. You therefore assign Universal Principles more realistically.

Finally, compare the General Principle(s) behind each option. Which is the most responsible General Principle(s) in this situation? The answer to this question comes as a result of weighing the General Principles that drive all the options.

Awareness and acknowledgment of differences; respect for traditions other than your own; changes in thinking and in initiatives; principled and responsible decisions flowing from a practical decision-making process—all these will help open the door to waiting opportunities.

It would be naive to think that all the differences and contradictions between our business and ethical systems can be overcome to the mutual satisfaction of all. Some differences will never be reconciled. No country or its businesspeople should have to sell out to another. But we have not been sensitive and open enough to business and ethical systems different from our own. While different from yours and mine in many ways, the cultures and customs of other countries are not beyond a working spirit of what we both would call, in our own ways, cooperation and shared moral responsibility.

## Finding Out About Yourself

If you or your organization does (or will be doing) business outside the United States, here are some good questions to answer:

1. Are you a U.S. businessperson or member of an organization that happens to do business overseas? Or are you a global businessperson or member of an organization that happens to have headquarters in the United States? What implications does your answer have for future activities?

   _____

   _____

   _____

   _____

2. Shorten your learning curve. What could you or your organization do in the next three months to learn more about the foreign people with whom you deal?

   _____

   _____

   _____

   _____

3. In each country where you are now involved, what particular ways in which they do business—values, customs, laws, and norms—are already "red flag" danger issues for you or your organization?

   _____

   _____

_____

_____

4. What specific ethical/legal business dilemmas are you now facing overseas?

_____

_____

_____

_____

5. What particular ideas from this chapter could help you solve dilemmas or begin more productive ways of doing business overseas?

_____

_____

_____

_____

# Note

1. Jeffrey A. Fadiman, "A Traveler's Guide to Gifts and Bribes," *Harvard Business Review* (July/August 1986), pp. 4–11. Copyright © 1986 by the President and Fellows of Harvard College; all rights reserved.

# 10

# How to Walk Your Talk

## Putting Ethics Systems in Organizations

The purpose of this book is to present the value-based decision-making process and urge your adoption of this valuable tool. The positive results are more effective, responsible, and justifiable decisions. The use of the process takes some learning and a good deal of practice until it becomes second nature.

But even more, use of the process as a core decision-making tool requires that it be backed up with mechanisms for applying it as a natural part of work routine. The process needs personal and organizational systems that support, nurture, and monitor its use.

I want you to look at some of those systems in the context of five implementation guidelines, which are accompanied, where possible, by examples of systems in use by organizations. These guidelines help you adopt and use the process itself. The systems examples mentioned in this chapter are used by medium-size and large organizations. You will have to consider how to adapt their structure and use for your own needs, size, and resources.

## Implementation Guidelines

### Mission and Purpose Statements

*Guideline 1: Identify business/ethical values and principles that are critical to your philosophy and operation.*[1] The first step is to be working "on purpose." Your mission and purpose statement defines who you are, where you are going, how you will get there, and the basic values and principles that drive your efforts. As seen in Chapter 3, primary business and moral values are usually embedded in the statement itself or listed directly afterward. Southwestern Bell succinctly identifies customer satisfaction, its people, quality, and integrity as primary values immediately following the mission statement. Nova Natural Resources Corporation, a small Colorado oil, gas, and mineral exploration company, repeatedly accentuates its values of creativity, risk, persistence, value, and honesty in the president's formal client presentations.

However formulated and publicized, your purpose, values, and working principles should be clear, official, and shared by all members. Such principles and values are the main factor in creating the organizational climate and culture, making decisions, and taking actions for success. The three-step process feeds your values and principles into the creation of your unique decisions. Policy and procedure manuals, codes of ethics, and training will mirror, amplify, explain, and apply these principles further.

> "I firmly believe that any organization, in order to survive and achieve success, must have a sound set of beliefs on which it premises all its policies and actions. Next, I believe that the most important single factor in corporate success is faithful adherence to those beliefs."
> —Thomas J. Peters and Robert H. Waterman, Jr.

## Interview and Selection Systems

*Guideline 2: Select employees with not only the needed business skills and attitudes, but also the desired ethical values and attitudes.* Business and ethical attitudes basic to fulfillment of your mission and purpose can be built into position advertising, job descriptions, and previews, as long as these attitudes are tied to job performance. This will probably be a new mode of operation for you and your organization; it will take some trial-and-error attempts, but it will be well worth the effort.

When verifying information on job applications and re-sumes, you should pay attention to what values and principles were displayed by applicants in previous work situations. Look between the lines for dedication, willingness to learn, openness to new ideas, and respect for stakeholders, among others.

Up-to-date interview models that are currently available provide settings in which values can be explored. Assessment center technology, work simulations, hands-on exercises, cases, and face-to-face interviews can seek out a candidate's values and how each candidate would apply personal and organizational principles in your business climate. Asking candidates how they managed situations in the past—"Tell me the story of what happened and how you handled it"—is revealing. Past behavior is a good predictor of future behavior. Objective testing and the resulting psychological profiles can be used as a tool in the selection process.

Properly used, a selection process that incorporates work-related business/ethical values and attitudes should not breach legal rights of privacy or equal opportunity employment requirements. This is generally true as long as values, attitudes, and the selection process are directly related to job performance. Current interview models, which you can purchase, often note which questions can and can't be asked of candidates.

Granted, such a focus requires somewhat subjective judgments not easily quantified, but giving weight to work-related values and attitudes regardless of race, religion, gender, national origin, and age should not violate discrimination laws.

## Performance and Evaluation Systems

*Guideline 3: Incorporate ethical values and attitudes in the work performance and evaluation process.* Job performance criteria that reflect shared principles influence employee behavior, particularly when the principles are not only mandated but seen as "the way of life, the way things are done around here." You saw some examples of shared values in Chapter 3: quality products, trust, respect for others, open communication, fairness to employees, integrity of record keeping, honesty and candor in all activities, freedom to make mistakes, profit as a means of measuring service, encouragement of initiative, and a public spirit. Care must be taken, though, to spell out concretely what these values mean in your operation.

Performance appraisals can then evaluate attainment of business goals and objectives in the light of ethical principles and attitudes. While the styles of conducting performance evaluations differ widely, they generally include the areas of information recording and reporting; protection of resources; conflicts of interest; workplace environment; management/employee relations; and relationships with customers, vendors, suppliers, competitors, and the community.

### Codes

Codes of ethics are now commonplace in organizations. Their styles vary, but they generally address fundamental guiding values and principles; workplace and product safety; environmental responsibility; employee privacy; confidentiality of employee records and corporate proprietary material; drug-related and discrimination issues; grievance procedures; and technological innovation, among others.

Codes are effective when they are compiled with as much participation as possible. "Buy-in" and willing compliance can then be better ensured. Even if a code is written only by top-level executives, "buy-in" from the ranks still must be gained at some point. Codes must be moved from mere commands to acceptance as part of a shared responsibility. All things being equal, they should not be formulated quickly and hastily by top management alone. A good code of ethics takes time, experience, care, and the input of many within the organization.

A workable code of ethics must have some other important characteristics as well. It must be fully understood by everyone. This takes time, energy, and patient education. A code should promote a free and open atmosphere for discussion, questions, differences, and reporting of violations without retaliation. Whistleblowers should be viewed and managed proactively as a valuable part of the company's open communication, feedback, and improvement efforts, not treated as disloyal adversaries. The consequences of violating the code and its standards must be fully explained and followed with fairness. Those responsible for monitoring and enforcing the code should be clearly designated and given authority to fulfill their functions.

### Team, Committee, and Advocacy Functions

Work teams and special committees can perform design, monitoring, and enforcement functions. They might even oversee ethics programs and procedures, interpret policies, and investigate violations.

Quality circles have been used in numerous companies for various purposes. I found an intriguing and challenging adaptation of the quality circle concept, called a "moral quality circle," that addresses ethical issues. It is the idea of a professor of anthropology, Lionel Tiger, of Rutgers University. His rationale points back millions of years to when hunters and gatherers, living in small groups, shaped their survival around an ethical system based on mutual need and cooperation. In that close, demanding environment of face-to-face dealings, there was no place to hide. He claims that people developed a kind of "gene for morality" and cooperation, which worked well until tribal ties weakened with the shift to an agricultural way of life. Commitment to cooperation weakened as well when it became possible to prosper at the expense of others. A new ethical approach gradually evolved with the rise of the dominant religions practiced today, but their ethical systems are more attuned to small shepherds and farmers than to the industrial and information ages of recent times. Tiger sees people in large organizations as less able to make moral judgments today because of the size and complexity of corporate life.

He suggests that the matter of corporate ethics be placed in the hands of small groups of employees at every level of the organization, where "morality genes" can still thrive in the setting of a quality circle. Tiger feels that such an arrangement will appeal to management and also have the virtue of bringing out the best in human nature—the part that's been millions of years in the making.

The role of ombudsman is often adopted by companies to foster ethical conduct. Ombudsmen "embody the corporate conscience," as one company puts it. Some ombudsmen (and women) listen to employee grievances, problems, and questions. They problem-solve by developing options that employees can choose to exercise, and by receiving information in confidence about breaches of ethics. They fact-find and investigate before employee decisions for action are taken, and they mediate between employees and others in the company. In some cases, they report facts to management for the purpose of policy changes. The Charles Schwab Corporation uses the services of an outside ombudsman to prevent the perception that he or she is "owned" by management.

Many organizations appoint special committees that formulate, promote, and monitor ethical standards and compliance. Honeywell, Inc., has a Corporate Committee on Ethics as part of its ethics program. Its function is to formulate and promote compliance with Honeywell's business conduct policies, provide direction to the ethics program, and ensure that employees, customers, and the public recognize the high priority Honeywell places on ethical business conduct.

The Defense Industry Initiative on Business Ethics and Conduct (DII) was formed in 1986 in response to the recommendations of the Reagan-appointed Packard Commission. Now grown to fifty-five signatories, including the top ten defense contractors, DII develops ethical business policies, procedures, and programs for implementation in six areas: codes of ethics; ethics training; self-governance systems to monitor procurement laws and adopt procedures for voluntary disclosure of violations; responsibility to the industry through special forums; and accountability to the public.[2] This industry-centered approach could be used by other industries and their professional associations.

### Audit Functions

Audits are internal systematic reviews of policies, procedures, and practices at specific operational levels, as well as regular examinations of select activities within an organization. Teams or committees often audit contracts, finances, and ethics together as a means of promoting and ensuring compliance with stated values and business policies.

Dow Corning Corporation (DCC) is a good example. In the

early 1970s, following Watergate and defense industry disclo-
sures, the IRS asked heads of U.S. corporations to answer
questions concerning bribes, gifts, slush funds, and "grease
payments." While considering the questions, Jack Ludington,
then the Dow Corning CEO, wanted to feel more confident that
his employees (many of whom were new and from cultures with
different ways of doing business) would live up to the high marks
of corporate responsibility he felt were earned at DCC. In 1976,
the board of directors appointed an Audit and Social Responsibility Committee (ASRC) to oversee certain aspects of the
company's internal and external activities. Two months later,
four senior managers were appointed to the first corporate
Business Conduct Committee (BCC), which reported to the
ASRC. Their task: to learn more about how the company oper-
ated outside the United States; develop guidelines for commu-
nicating legal and ethical standards of conduct around the world;
develop a process for monitoring and reporting the company's
business practices; and recommend ways to correct questionable practices as they became known.

A corporate code of conduct was developed and revised
over time to allow specific interpretations for specific needs in
different cultures overseas. To communicate the code, the BCC
began a series of annual audits, conducted with managers worldwide. This audit process evolved over the years, but it typically
involved dialogues about gray areas, briefings on issues related
to the code of conduct, and wide-ranging discussions on key
topics. Discussion often included such topics as competitors,
government, customer relations, distributor practices, pricing,
questionable payments, importing procedures, and employee
concerns. DCC used the audits to clarify and revise its code,
communicate it to employees, inform all its employees about
company activities, and update training. By 1983, a separate
BCC began functioning like an ombudsman, reviewing record-
keeping issues, performance review systems, older-employee
issues, sexual harassment policies, and restrictions on accepting
gifts and gratuities.[3]

The role of Johnson & Johnson's audit group is to advise,
monitor, and investigate. It participates in establishing the policy of Business Conduct, advises management on ethical issues,
monitors the Business Conduct policy, performs special investi-

gations where needed, and monitors management's enforcement of the Business Conduct policy.

Medtronic's code of business conduct demands strict compliance with laws and regulations; it strongly prohibits political contributions, bribes, kickbacks, and other payments for illegal purposes. It orders books and records to accurately reflect all transactions, designating the general counsel as the reporting point for deviations. To monitor its code, Medtronic has an internal audit function as a key corporate policy; the function is charged with independently appraising all aspects of the company's activities worldwide. The corporate audit department reports to management and to the audit committee of the board.[4]

Through a series of self-report statements, a type of survey audit measures the ethical climate of an organization as perceived by individuals connected to the organization in some way. One such instrument is the *Organizational Integrity Perception Audit.*[5] It measures two perceptions of the participant: the actual ethical climate in his or her organization, and the desired climate. The difference between the desired climate and the perceived reality yields a "gap score" that indicates possible problem areas in the organization. With some indexing and weighting, gap scores are translated into an aggregate score and compared to the score of a control group. "Interacting responsibly" and "modeling integrity" are two of the organizational cluster areas measured. Sample statements include "People are treated fairly" (a Likert scale of desired and actual is marked); "People freely admit their mistakes"; and "Alternative courses of action are considered in dealing with an ethical problem."

*Training Resources*

Organizational training functions are a key ingredient in implementing and applying ethical values and principles, especially when using this decison-making process. Training in ethics should have significant priority; ethics should be taught as a practical skill on the same level as other business skills. The ethics training program at Honeywell, Inc., is an example of a developed, decision-centered, behavior-based curriculum. Delivered in phases from 1986 to 1989, it's made up of topical and policy training, supervisory and management development, and a leadership conference—each category focused on a particular audience. Unlike many other training programs, Honeywell's policy training emphasizes ethical decision making, the use of performance appraisals, reinforcement of policies and procedures, the use of consultants, and first-workday, new-employee orientation. Supervisory and management development includes, among other things, a one-day module that focuses on resolution of ethical dilemmas, employee motivation, and the "3 Rs" (recognize the issue, raise the issue, and resolve the issue). The leadership conference, for all vice-presidents and above, presents ethics and values in the context of a leadership model.[6] A fully developed program like Honeywell's may not be possible for smaller organizations. But you should mandate and provide some training in value-based decision making and principled behaviors at a level you need and can afford.

## Recognition and Reward Systems

*Guideline 4: Establish a work climate now—and nurture a culture for the future—that reinforces and rewards ethical attitudes.* You, and management at all levels of an organization, can do much to establish a climate and form an organizational culture that fosters the primacy of ethical attitudes and behaviors. One important way you can exert influence is to build ethics into the recognition and reward system, especially if ethical attitudes and principles are already a part of selection, expected behavior, training, and audits. Employees don't simply do what they are told to do; they do what they want to do. Edicts without explanation and rationale are not true motivators, and they give birth to negative work norms rather than official, shared standards. People tend to act in consonance with standards they have helped decide, have accepted as their own, and are rewarded for. What you need is commitment, not just compliance.

Recognition and rewards need not always be financial. I have heard hundreds of managers and salespeople express the earnest desire to be recognized publicly and individually in other ways. Examples include an award, a ceremony with family and colleagues present, a private letter from supervisors or the CEO, spoken thanks, or a special, sought-after privilege. Positive reinforcement—given immediately for specific behaviors—is more powerful and lasting than punishment for misbehavior. Nonetheless, ethical productivity as well as regular productivity should be reflected in compensation and promotion policies as well.

## Management Modeling

*Guideine 5: Exhibit ethical leadership.* One characteristic is without doubt absolutely essential: You must model the organizational purpose, values, and business principles, as well as your own. Most of all, model your moral principles within the moral attitude of responsibility—the heart of the three-step process.

Nothing will happen, nothing will be better or different, unless that modeling is routinely present—at every level of operation, all the time, and for everyone to see. The ethics of an organization will never be better than your own ethics. Phony PR for public consumption won't do the job. Changing the ground rules in private for "special crunches" won't wash. Executive adeptness at inconsistency for short-term success puts long-term success at risk. Sheer expediency without moral uneasiness will eventually bring trouble. Organizational members and the public aren't that professionally illiterate today, if they ever were. And stakeholder sophistication has a way of conducting its own "audit process."

We live and work in the gray zone; you and I, like the world, are far from perfect. Will we make mistakes, even big ones? Sure. Mistakes can be forgiven, remedied, and used as learning experiences—if intentions are first aligned with good purpose.

We must walk our talk.

Every better value-based decision you make—and the best one possible—is a positive and exciting step further into a world filled with both opportunity and promise.

# Notes

1. Guidelines adapted from Robert W. Goddard, "Are You an Ethical Manager? *Personnel Journal* (March 1988). Used with permission of *Personnel Journal,* Costa Mesa, California; all rights reserved.

2. Alan Yuspeh, *Defense Industry Initiative on Business Ethics and Conduct: 1990 Annual Report to the Public and the Defense Industry,* 1991.
3. "Dow Corning Corporation: Business Conduct and Global Values," a case study by David Whiteside, *Harvard Business School,* copyright 1984, by the President and Fellows of Harvard College; all rights reserved.
4. *Medtronics, Inc.: Key Global Corporate Policies,* Medtronics, Inc., 1991.
5. Doug Wallace and Julie Belle White, *Organizational Integrity Perception Audit* (St. Paul: The College of St. Catherine, 1987).
6. "Integrating Business Ethics Conference" (Presentation on the Honeywell Ethics Program, The Conference Board, April 24, 1991).

# Index